T0122178

TOO GREAT A NATION
AMERICA'S LAST CHANCE

by
Dan Fragoules

Order this book online at www.trafford.com
or email orders@trafford.com

Most Trafford titles are also available at major online book retailers.

© Copyright 2009 Dan Fragoules.
All rights reserved. No part of this publication may be reproduced, stored in a retrieval system, or
transmitted, in any form or by any means, electronic, mechanical, photocopying, recording, or
otherwise, without the written prior permission of the author.

Printed in Victoria, BC, Canada.

ISBN: 978-1-4269-2137-7 (sc)
ISBN: 978-1-4269-2138-4 (hc)

Library of Congress Control Number: 2009941117

*Our mission is to efficiently provide the world's finest, most comprehensive book publishing
service, enabling every author to experience success. To find out how to publish your book, your
way, and have it available worldwide, visit us online at www.trafford.com*

Trafford rev. 11/24/09

 www.trafford.com

North America & international
toll-free: 1 888 232 4444 (USA & Canada)
phone: 250 383 6864 ✦ fax: 812 355 4082

Contents

Contents

INTRODUCTION

The American experiment succeeded beyond the wildest expectations of our founding fathers. They threw off the chains of British Monarchy, bound the thirteen colonies under a representative government, and unleashed the power of a free and self-interested people; the power of an individual with the chance to make a better place in the world for himself and his family, multiplied many times. It's a human potential that had never quite been allowed an opportunity before. It is the force that catapulted not just this nation but the human race from black powder to space travel.

As a group, the American people perform predictably. Given opportunity we prosper, when challenged we fight, take away our incentive and we get lazy. This is the greatest country in the world because free and prosperous people work harder to earn, and fight harder to keep, the wealth and power necessary to preserve a nation. Wealth is what made this country strong and it is the only thing that will keep it strong. The source of our wealth is the individual self interest that comes with freedom. And while that wealth has preserved our nation against every military and economic challenge for over two hundred years, it is the Declaration of Independence and the United States Constitution that protects our freedom; not from foreign armies, but from our own leaders, who from the very beginning has been a mix of greatness, mediocrity, incompetence, and criminal.

There are those to whom we owe our liberty and prosperity. And there are those whose decisions perpetrated almost a hundred years of slavery, a civil war, and the great depression. Our short history has shown that self rule can pay huge dividends, and that we pay a high price for poor leadership. Today our leaders are ignoring the principles in these documents, and as a result have started our nation on the downward slide familiar to all of history's empires. This was the greatest experiment in the history of mankind. It is special, but it is not invincible.

The future of our country is being threatened, not by Islamic extremist or Iranian nuclear weapons, but by 552 people in our government who are selling legislation and policy to multinational corporations and special interest groups. It's not political ideology, it's a massive theft motivated by greed and perpetrated by self-important lawmakers, both republican and democrat. There is a point past which it will not be possible to recover, an amount they can spend that just cannot be repaid. If we fail to act now, if we let this continue until our economic system collapses, the aftermath will be violent. We will be committing someone to fight again for freedom in America. Our children are going to suffer for our mistakes in the best case, but if a war must be fought to save this country, we have a moral obligation not to leave it for them to fight.

The genius of our system is that it put the ruling power in the hands of the states and the people. The real danger in what's happening today is the shifting of that power. Every day that the government becomes more powerful we become less free. Freedom, the one thing that makes this country the last greatest hope for mankind on earth, is slipping from our grasp; well, not really slipping from our grasp, it's being stolen from under our noses because we are not fighting to keep it.

We are being asked to accept the accelerating expansion of the Federal Government on the theory that they are smarter than we are; that the people, in control of their state and local governments, need an expert from Washington to tell us how to educate our children, build our homes, and spend our money. The genius of our founding documents came from the common sense of the men who wrote them. It doesn't work the other way around. You seldom get common sense from a genius. And you never get common sense from government; it is fundamentally incompatible with bureaucracy.

The Constitution is designed to allow the people to control their government at the state and local level, and to limit the role of the

Federal Government to that of overseeing interaction between states and to protecting the states. Our leaders today have forgotten that we fought the revolutionary war against too much government. Most of them apparently do not understand the connection between a free people and a prosperous society, that each is necessary for the other to exist.

We are deep in debt and no tax rate will bring in enough money to make the payments. We have to make a choice, either quit spending money on anything that's not necessary and start paying down this debt, or just keep spending, knowing that a bankruptcy is coming in any case. That's where our country is right now and the choice is ours. Making the right choice will not be easy, but we will pay a very high price if we don't. It's a mathematical equation that has been tested many times, always returning the same result. Too much national debt plus continuing to spend more than you have equals economic collapse. It happened in 1789 France, 1917 Russia, and 1933 Germany, and the result was bodies in the street.

The decision we make here will affect the lives of generations to come as profoundly as did the founding itself. This is *Too Great a Nation* for us to make the wrong choice.

> *"You and I have a rendezvous with destiny. We will preserve for our children this, the last best hope of man on earth, or we will sentence them to take the last step into a thousand years of darkness. If we fail, at least let our children and our children's children say of us we justified our brief moment here. We did all that could be done."* - **Ronald Reagan**

> *"Rightful liberty is unobstructed action according to our will within limits drawn around us by the equal rights of others. I do not add 'within the limits of the law' because law is often but the tyrant's will, and always so when it violates the rights of the individual."* - **Thomas Jefferson**

THE HONEST CHOICE

When our forefathers won independence for these United States, it gave its citizens the opportunity to go to work, start businesses, make things, mine things and grow things. In an amazingly short time we built the most powerful economy the world has ever seen. The government is dependent on our productivity and that cannot be turned around. We cannot be dependent on the government because the government does not, and cannot, produce. If our system provides incentive for productive behavior, the American people will produce, which will grow the economy and provide more opportunity, more production, and tax revenue.

It is a simple system but there are real limits that the government has to stay within to keep it working. The government has a responsibility, in its own self interest, as well as in ours, not to be a burden to our productivity. But in a free society productive people are independent people and that is not compatible with the expanding role of the Federal Government.

In 1953 over 28 percent of the U.S. workforce was employed by manufacturers[1]. Today there are more Americans employed by the Federal Government than by the manufacturing and construction industries combined[2]. This is no accident. Our leaders are intentionally promoting policies that move people out of the productive segment of our society and into one form or another of government dependency because it increases their power.

The Constitution is designed to prevent a big central government. When social policy is set at the state level, the societies that work well influence those who don't and competition puts pressure on poorly performing states to improve. The diversity leads to innovation as public policy evolves to meet the changing circumstances of an advancing society. It is obvious from our history that this model works; it's also obvious that the big central government model does not.

The growth of the Federal Government is out of control, and the bigger it gets the more poorly it performs. Without discipline it will keep growing until it collapses under its own weight. There is no competitive pressure to change bad policy or to discontinue failing programs. The only thing that can discipline it is the electorate. But the American people are no longer in control of that process. We have had no choice since the two major parties took over the election process. They have both systematically moved power from the people to the government and the special interests that support them.

Our nation and our liberty are ours to lose. Ben Franklin is said to have said "a republic if you can keep it" when ask what kind of government they had made for us. He knew that we would have to be proactive, that the Constitution would not defend itself. Our nation is at a crossroads and if we are going make the honest choice, we must first retrieve our right to do so.

The only thing that protects America's representative government is the rule of law. The longer we allow our government to take actions, for which it has no legal authority, the harder it will be for us to exercise our Constitutional sovereignty over it. The Federal Government as it operates today is unconstitutional and unsustainable. The only way to salvage our representative system is for it to return to or be replaced by the limited government outlined in the Constitution.

There is a fundamental defect in our political structure that is eroding the representative nature of our system and is at the root of every problem we face. The offices of President, Senator, and Representative which are supposed to be by the people, for the people, and of the people are instead full time fundraising machines: by the money, for the money, and of the money. The first step in considering a serious run for one of these offices is to form an exploratory committee to determine if enough money can be raised. The fundraising never stops, and it necessarily changes the loyalties of the office holder from the good of the people to the good of the contributor.

The banking/housing crisis brought our economy to its knees early in 2009. In the 2008 election cycle securities and investment firms, commercial banks, mortgage companies and insurers gave 143 million dollars to the 535 members of Congress.

The Social Security/Medicare system is insolvent. In the 2008 election cycle 535 members of Congress received more than 127 million dollars from corporations and lobbying groups who profit from these programs.

Excessive litigation costs our economy 800 billion dollars a year. In the 2008 election cycle lawyers gave 124 million dollars to the 535 members of Congress[2].

In 2009 the economy showed the first signs of collapsing under the weight of increasing government spending and debt that was supported by an ever smaller segment of productive society. Congress and President Obama took advantage of the opportunity to pass an 800 billion taxpayer dollar stimulus package that spent more money on the National Endowment for the Arts than it did to help small business. Each member of Congress who voted for it exchanged their support for getting a share of the money to their own special interest. Just when we needed to cut spending, they instead added another permanent layer of bureaucracy that will have to be funded again in each succeeding budget.

When in 2009 Congress began the debate over health care reform, hundreds of millions of dollars came pouring into Washington from organizations planning to profit from their influence over the decision making process. They get what they pay for - that's how we got 12 trillion dollars in debt in the first place. And what did they pay for? A two thousand page bill that leaves in place the whole failed system that will still bankrupt this nation.

Any reasonable group of people could reform our health care system in five or ten pages. The founding fathers wrote the rules for the entire United States government in four or five pages. There is no excuse for even considering a document that is so complex that even its authors don't understand its practical ramifications.

Our country was founded as an experiment in self rule, but it is now being run by a ruling class of professional politicians more closely resembling royalty than citizen leaders. The transfer of power was not a complicated process. The act of spending itself moves power from citizens to government, because the government has no money of its own. In July of 2009, as our country teetered on the brink of insolvency, the House of Representatives illustrated their arrogance by voting to spend 332 million dollars on luxury Gulf Stream jets to be used by members of Congress. This should have been the last straw, but with so many last straws lying around it probably won't make any difference.

Only a handful of people whose connection to the American people has been severed by the power and wealth of their positions are in control of this country. They are oblivious to the fact that, constitutionally, it is not their power, it is ours. And if we don't take it back we will all find ourselves starting over in a place that bears no resemblance to the United States of America.

552 people – the President, the Vice President, the 15 heads of executive departments, 100 Senators and 435 Representatives – are all we have to replace to take back our government.

These professional politicians want us to believe that the problems are too complex for us to understand. But the problem is politicians who believe they should serve for life, who no longer answer to the American people, and who don't understand or follow the Constitution they have taken an oath to defend.

There is a pent up desire in the American public for the kind of honest common sense government that this country was founded on. In 1992 we would have defeated the presidential candidates of both parties if Ross Perot had not self destructed or whatever it was that happened to him. In 2008 Barack Obama won by default because he was the closest thing to "not the same" on the ballot. After he picked her, John McCain decided that Sarah Palin was not smart enough to be his Vice President, but we have elected the smart people for 20 years and look where it got us.

We do not need John McCain, Barack Obama, or anyone else that has taken part in the rape and pillage of our right to self rule. This country has had all the experts it can afford, it's time to send the lawyers and economist home and hire small businessmen, homebuilders, electricians, and yes, even plumbers, to replace them.

It's our country, and we can take it back. You don't need to be a lawyer or have a degree to run for office. In the next election every member of the House of Representatives could be replaced in one day. It won't be easy because they have money, power, and they are in control of the election process. But it is necessary.

Vote for no incumbent, particularly in the primaries. Both parties are part of the problem. Each party has interest of its own, and collect's hundreds of millions of dollars from people with interest of their own. They will be behind the incumbent in each primary. If they can be defeated in the primary it will throw out a bum without merely rewarding the other party. Independent and third party candidates would be better but the important thing is for every incumbent to lose. The very few members of congress who do honestly fight for our Constitution, will be glad to give up their seats if the American people will stand up and take this country back.

Congress has illegally seized the power that belongs to the people and it will be hard, maybe impossible to retrieve. So in order to restore the representative nature of our government, we the people should go over the heads of Congress and propose for consideration by the states five amendments to the Constitution.

1. A balanced budget Amendment.

2. An Amendment establishing term limits in both houses of Congress

3. An Amendment requiring Congress to pass legislation and funding for each project or program one item at a time, rather than bundling billions of dollars in pork with every bill. This would also require the President to sign off on each item. There is no reason we should be forced to accept ten dollars worth of spending we don't want for every one dollar we need. Under our current system Congress spends money on such a wholesale basis that it is impossible for them to even read what they are voting for, or more importantly, to take responsibility for it. When they have to vote on each spending item one at a time, they will only be able to pass thirty or forty each day. That's plenty.

4. An Amendment modernizing the line in Article I Section VIII which gives Congress the power "To establish Post Offices and post Roads". It should be amended to state that Congress has the power "To regulate and enforce the security of document delivery and transmission within the United States, its territories, and appropriate foreign locations. The reason we need to do this now is to make a point. The power to establish the post office was granted in the Constitution because it was explicitly not within the government's authority otherwise. This is the precedent that all other government agencies should be held to. If they would not have had the authority to create the Postal Service without specific authorization, then any like organization is similarly illegal. Also in 1787 this was a large unsettled country with no other communication than the post and it would have been hard to hold together without it. Today the job of delivering information, documents, funds, and parcels is being done more efficiently and securely by private companies. Add the fact that the Post Office lost 1.1 billion taxpayer dollars in the second quarter of 2009 alone and it becomes obvious that the government should get out of this business.

5. An Amendment defining a process for allowing the people to bypass Congress and propose popular amendments. There are two ways spelled out in the Constitution for how to propose an amendment. The first is for a bill to pass both houses of the legislature, by a two-thirds majority in each. Once the bill has passed both houses, it goes on to the states. The second method is for a Constitutional Convention to be called by two-thirds of the legislatures of the States. Since this method has never been used it is probably not a workable way for the people to bypass Congress, which was its intent. Although not spelled out in the Constitution, the idea of a popular amendment is consistent with the principles in the Constitution. It derives its power from the people, and it functions on behalf of the people, so the state legislatures would be obligated to consider amendments that were proposed by the people. We the People could circulate and sign these petitions and send them

directly to the states for ratification, bypassing a Congress that no longer represents our interests.

We have a right to expect Congress to operate within the law and obey the Constitution. Starting with the 10th amendment, which says "the powers not delegated to the United States by the Constitution, nor prohibited by it to the States, are reserved to the States respectively, or to the people". Of the over 1300 Federal Government Departments and Agencies, most do not fall within the powers granted to the Federal Government, and are not, when you consider the cost, a benefit to the people. It is not within the Federal Government's Constitutional role to be in the health insurance, passenger train, banking, automobile manufacturing, or retirement fund business.

The Constitution gives each of these United States all of the power not specifically granted to the Federal Government. It is time for each state to stand up for its rights. Your State Government has the Constitutional authority to check the Federal Government. We must refuse to allow the Federal Government to impose laws for which they have no authority. It is the right and the responsibility of your governor and state legislature to keep the Federal Government within its legal bounds.

The Federal Government is expanding into roles for which it has no authority while at the same time it is failing in its constitutionally mandated responsibilities. Article IV Section IV of the Constitution requires Congress and the President to stop the invasion of criminals who are entering this country from Mexico. It reads in part; "The United States shall protect each of them [states] against Invasion; and on Application of the Legislature, or of the Executive (when the Legislature cannot be convened) against domestic Violence". There is nothing wrong with Mexicans immigrating to America, but there is something very wrong with having no control over how many drug dealers, terrorist, and child rapist enters our country illegally.

We deserve a government that honestly and legally represents our interests, and takes seriously their obligations and limitations under the Constitution. A government that would disentangle itself from our lives and leave to the states, armed with the legal authority to do so the task of making law.

Like laws reforming a legal system that is suffocating our economy. When a company fails, its assets should be preserved for the people who own them, not stolen by a court system that is designed to divert the assets into the pockets of lawyers at the expense of the creditors, suppliers, and employees that our system should protect.

And laws that say that anyone receiving public money, whether it's a Senator's salary or a welfare check, must pass a drug test. It is wrong to take money from taxpayers and allow it to support the untaxed, underground drug trade and then tax us again to fight drugs and related crime. Of course all drug laws will be state laws since nowhere in the constitution does it say that the Federal Government can tell the states what substances they may or may not prohibit.

And most important of all, because it is wrong to allocate public funds based on who pays the biggest bribes, we do need a federal law that clearly states that it is illegal for any candidate for, or holder of, any federal office to take money or favors from any organization, directly or indirectly, under penalty of imprisonment. This means we have to change how we elect our public officials.

Anyone who wants to run for a federal office should submit a resume to the American people they wish to represent at least two years prior to Election Day, and a comprehensive statement of policy, or platform, at least one year prior to Election Day. These documents should be published on web sites set up exclusively for this purpose, and made available at court houses and libraries. Both formats would provide the people the means to add their names to a petition of support to each candidate they agree with. Any candidate who receives the support of two percent of the eligible electorate will then be given access to public campaign funds. This will be the only money they are allowed to spend on their campaigns other than their own money which will be limited to two hundred thousand dollars, for a Presidential candidate, per election, adjusted annually for inflation.

Candidates for other federal offices would follow the same process with resumes and policy statements being posted in the areas to be represented, and with lower personal spending limits. Although it is not the Federal Government's role to tell anyone how they can or cannot spend their money, in this case there is too much room for corruption. Anyone's money could be moved into your income stream for political purposes.

The power and influence of the two major parties has been gained at the expense of the voter. They have divided us into blue and red camps to limit our choices. They have divided us by race and income to pit us against each other. They are part of the campaign financing, power to the contributor corruption that must stop. This plan would eliminate primary elections in favor of more choices in the general election where we could narrow the field for run-off elections.

It does fall within the government's Constitutional responsibility to insure our right to choose our leaders, so public funding of campaigns is a necessary evil. It is Congress's responsibility to appropriate the funds and the Federal Election Commission should distribute them with everything open and every dime published before Election Day.

Once our government is required to act within its legal authority there will be no government sponsored television. PBS will survive if enough people want to support it, not because the Federal Government forced enough people to support it. However, the Federal Election Commission may need to provide a forum for candidates to air their views if the national media fails to do so.

In the free society that we will save, you will only need one thing to be successful, and it is worth more than money, education, or even hard work: Honor. If you are trustworthy, honest, and dependable, the world is yours. Banks will loan you money, employers will give you responsibility, and customers will buy your products and service. They will tell their friends, more people will trust you, and your value grows.

We should be teaching our children the value of honor. Without honor anything else we give them is worthless. With honor they can have anything they want. But instead our system seems designed to do the opposite. The process by which we elect our political leaders leaves no room for honor in government and the incentives that many government programs promote in our society place no value on honor.

This country is more important than the people who hold office in Washington. It's more important than the health, wealth, and comfort of its citizens. Americans have sacrificed time and again for this truth. In our unencumbered People lies the potential to change the destiny of our species. The American Revolution was a once in the history of mankind opportunity, if we blow this there may never be another chance.

It will be an uphill battle, and success is not assured. So the last thing that Common Sense dictates that we do is prepare for the worst. Sell some stock, cash in your savings, sell your toys, and buy guns and ammunition, food, and water. Because America is worth fighting for and there is a point past which it will not be saved without a fight.

> *"We hold these truths to be self-evident, that all men are created equal, that they are endowed by their Creator with certain unalienable Rights, --that among these are Life, Liberty and the pursuit of Happiness. --That to secure these rights, Governments are instituted among Men, deriving their just powers from the consent of the governed, --That whenever any Form of Government becomes destructive of these ends, it is the Right of the People to alter or to abolish it, and to institute new Government."* - **The Declaration of Independence**

SPENDING AND TAXES

Government is vital to our society. We need it to defend our freedom, represent our interest abroad, protect us from foreign aggression, and enforce laws and regulations. It operates programs and agencies without which we could not watch a weather forecast, purchase fresh and uncontaminated food, or make a bank deposit. Some things like national defense, space exploration, the internet, or GPS navigation just could not be done without centralized control. But it can destroy our society if we don't keep it under control.

The Constitution reserves to the states all of the power not specifically delegated to the Federal Government because the people have more control over their State Government. It is harder for a State Government to spend our money against our will. If a state's government becomes too oppressive you can move to another state. If the Federal Government becomes too oppressive there is no escape, if you can't escape, you are no longer free.

When the Federal Government sends money to the states, it is bypassing the vote of the people in that state. If the people of your state vote against a tax increase to improve your roads, the Federal Government then has no legal authority to over-ride your vote, to tax you, and to send the money back to your state to fix your roads anyway. Worse than that, if the people in my state vote against raising taxes to fix our roads, the Federal Government will tax people in another state, who did not have a vote and do not drive on our roads, and send the money to my state and fix our roads. And, in the event that we do vote for state taxes to fix our roads, we can see the results. When the Federal Government taxes us to fix roads, 9 out of every 10 dollars never makes it to the road.

Tax rates are a tool that the government uses to influence our behavior. They have no relation to what our share of the expense of government is. The only thing that determines what our burden will be is how much they spend. The Federal Government spent over 3 trillion dollars in 2009 with a deficit of close to 2 Trillion bringing the total debt to over $12 trillion dollars[1]. That's over $35,000 per man, woman and child in the United States.

This debt will increase at an escalating rate automatically because we are adding the interest on the debt to the debt. That is what will determine how much of your wealth it will be necessary to give up in support of your government. When government spending increases, its income increases automatically, it's just a matter of how they get it. It's real spending and real debt, and they can't make it go away. They can borrow it, or print it, but in the end we will pay for it.

The idea that the government can "provide" is a myth that they are still propagating, and we are still swallowing, in spite of the obvious evidence to the contrary. The private sector is the only place where wealth is created. The only way government gets money is to take it from people who earn it. So it is physically impossible for the government to bail out the economy. It's like bailing a sinking boat while pouring the water back into the vessel. We are sinking because there is too much spending and not enough taxpaying.

The only way to collect more taxes is to create more private sector jobs. Public jobs aren't the answer because those wages are paid with federal spending; the boat is still sinking. Our private sector economy is shedding jobs at an escalating rate while the Federal Government is hiring more people and sending money to state and local governments so they can hire more people. They are financing all this with borrowed money.

Since it is obvious that there are not enough people left to pay it back, they should have run out of credit by now. But they are covertly buying their own treasury bonds to keep up the appearance that they are still worth something. This scheme cannot possibly work for long. The only ones that can save this country are the American people and if we don't restore the incentives that drive economic growth, there is nothing the government can do to avoid bankruptcy.

Since 1970, The Federal Government has run a deficit for all but four years (1998–2001) which makes Bill Clinton the only modern President to have balanced the budget. That was an opportunity; all George W. Bush had to do was submit a balanced budget each year and he could have forced the debate to be "what are we going to cut to pay for this?" Instead we spent a half trillion dollars on interest in 2008. Every decision made by the President or Congress should pass one test: *Is this in the best interest of the American people?* Instead, we have decisions being made by people who have taken millions of dollars from groups with interest of their own.

Our government has spent trillions of dollars bailing out people who would have been the subject of justice department investigations were it not for the fact that Bush, Obama, their treasury secretary's, and almost every member of Congress were financially involved. Our government has become destructive to the governed, and it's time that we exercise our right to alter or abolish it. Congress will not balance their budget unless we force them. They're spending money that's not theirs, and they don't have the discipline to do it responsibly.

In his 1776 pamphlet "Common Sense", Thomas Paine wrote about the distinction between society and government "they are not only different, but have different origins. Society is produced by our wants, and government by our wickedness; the former promotes our happiness POSITIVELY by uniting our affections, the latter NEGATIVELY by restraining our vices. The one encourages intercourse, the other creates distinctions. The first is a patron, the last a punisher". He then said that government is a necessary evil because "we find it necessary to surrender up a part of our property to furnish means for the protection of the rest".

The attempt to turn the government into a benefactor can only end in failure because government is not a source. Whatever it is that we want to do in our society, the discussion has to begin with the knowledge that the government cannot give it to us. The lesson we will learn is an old one, you get nothing for nothing. By what illogic have we decided that we would be better off taking from our fellow citizens than we would be if we provided for ourselves, is hard to fathom.

A certain level of public spending is necessary to protect, and beneficial to, a free people. The level of spending that we are seeing today will cause the end of the United States of America as a free society. We lost that freedom when we allowed the Federal Government to usurp the state's role as the seat of power. The Federal Government has become a powerful entity of its own that represents its own interest and sells legislation to the highest bidder. We are pretending that the government has something to give us, but it can give us nothing. All it can do is move something from one person or group of people to another.

The bureaucracy is expensive and inefficient. For every dollar's worth of benefit it provides, it consumes two. For every person it employs it must consume the earnings of two private sector employees. For a generation, Congress has succeeded in convincing each segment of the electorate that they would tax the other to pay for their spending. If they were doing their job "to collect taxes and spend it for the people's benefit" honestly, they would not have to lie to us.

INCOME TAXES

Any politician who tells you he is going to cut federal taxes is lying to you, unless he is going to cut spending and balance the budget. If he tells you he will cut your taxes by raising taxes on corporations, he's lying to you. What corporations charge for their product is a balance between the need to make a profit and the need to compete. The less you can charge and still make a profit, the more successful your company will be. When you tax a corporation, the cost goes directly to the price of the product and you pay it when you buy that product.

If he tells you that he is going to cut your taxes by raising taxes on the rich, he's lying to you. The rich have never paid taxes, and even if they did there's not enough money in all the rich pockets to pay for this level of spending, even if the rate was 100 percent. There are just not enough rich people. But there are enough middle class and poor people, there are millions of us. That's why they tax gas, cigarettes and beer. That's why most Social Security and Medicare taxes are paid by middle class working people. And that's why they hide half of those taxes from you. Another way the government funds its excess spending is to just print money, which devalues all the money including your pay check. It's as direct a tax as taking it out of your pocket. The only way our taxes will ever really be cut is to reduce the governments need for money.

A fair and honest tax code would increase government revenue by stimulating the economy. When Reagan took office in 1981, Federal revenues were about 500 billion, and the top tax rate was 70% He cut taxes to 15 and 28 percent and eliminated most deductions. By 1988 Federal revenues had increased to almost a trillion dollars. And the proportion of total income taxes paid by the top 1 percent of wage earners rose from 18 percent in 1981 to 28 percent in 1988[2]. It makes sense that there is a limit to how high taxes can go without damaging the economy. And that revenue will decrease when the economy slows. If your goal was to collect the most money you possibly could, the trick would be to find the highest effective level of taxation. In our Republic, however, the limit should have something to do with the point at which the cost of government exceeds the benefit to its citizens.

The US tax code is over sixteen thousand, eight hundred pages long. It would take a year to read, and a team of tax lawyers and accountants to work. Who do you think pays the taxes under that system? Well, it's not rich people with lawyers and accountants. And it's no accident. This system was designed by rich people, lawyers, and accountants, to enrich themselves and make everyone else foot the bill. The only reason for this over-complicated tax code is to hide that fact. They use smoke and mirrors to make it look like the bottom half of wage earners are paying no taxes so that they won't care what the tax rate is or how it's being spent.

The truth is that in 2008 the bottom 50% of wage earners paid 15.24% of their income in Social Security and Medicare taxes alone. Higher income earners paid only 2.9% on everything over $102,000[3]. The American people would never put up with this level of taxation if it was done out in the open. That's why the first step in reform is a simple, honest tax code. We need to take the lawyers and the accountants out of the process. And we need to turn the system around so that our government is accountable to us and not the other way around.

The federal budget should be related to federal revenue: their budget and our tax return should be basically the same document. The tax code should have two sections, the taxpaying section and the tax spending section. The taxpaying section is where we calculate how much to pay, with no mirrors, no hidden halves. You write your gross income on line one, write the first ten thousand on line 2, the zero percent line. Everyone's first ten thousand dollars of income would be tax free. Income over ten thousand up to one hundred thousand goes on line 3, the twenty percent line. The rest of your income up to five million dollars goes on the thirty percent line. And everything over that goes on the last, forty percent line. Then total the right hand column, the percentages for each line, and carry it to the spending section.

The spending section will have one line for each spending category with the percentage of the budget to be spent for that line. We should each calculate how much of our taxes will be spent for each category; it's the least we can do if we are going to keep an eye on how these people spend our money. Using 2008 spending percentages this tax form would look like this;

Taxing:

Gross Income	$200,000		Tax
First $10,000 of Income	$10,000	0%	0
Income over $10,000 but under $100,000	$90,000	20%	$18,000
Income over $100,000 but under 5,000,000	$100,000	30%	$30,000
Income over $5,000,000	$0	40%	0
Total Tax Liability			$48,000

Spending:

Social Security	21%	$10,080.00
Defense	21%	$10,080.00
★Medicare, Medicaid, and SCHIP	20%	$9,600.00
Unemployment/Welfare	11.2%	$5,376.00
Interest on Debt	9.0 %	$4,320.00
Miscellaneous Unidentified Spending	4.1%	$1,968.00
Health and Human Services	2.4%	$1,152.00
Department of Education	1.9%	$912.00
Department of Veterans Affairs	1.4%	$672.00
Department of Housing and Urban Development	1.2%	$576.00
State Department	1.2%	$576.00
Homeland Security	1.2%	$576.00
Department of Energy	.8%	$384.00
Department of Justice	.7%	$336.00
Department of Agriculture	.7%	$336.00
NASA	.6%	$288.00
Department Transportation	.4%	$192.00
Department Treasury	.4%	$192.00
Department Interior	.4%	$192.00
Department Labor	.4%	$192.00
Total		$48,000.00

★This line should be replaced by the Healthcare Voucher System outlined in chapter three.

At first glance this looks like a tax increase on lower income Americans, but that's just because I took out the lies. This system would actually raise taxes on the rich and cut taxes for most working people and small businesses. Here are some examples.

If you make:	2009 tax code	new plan
$30,000	$7,672	$4,000
$50,000	$12,670	$8,000
$75,000	$19005	$13,000
$100,000	$30,240	$18,000
$200,000	$48,386	$48,000
$500,000	$103,386	$120,000
$1,000,000	Nobody knows	$288,000
$5,000,000	Nobody knows	$1,488,000

Of Course, the 2009 tax code numbers are estimates because with a sixteen thousand page tax code, nobody knows for sure what tax you might pay on a six figure income. The important thing about this new system is that it is honest and uncomplicated. It puts everybody in the game, playing by the same rules. No deductions, no hidden taxes, no accountants or tax lawyers. If you think forty percent is too high for a top rate, think about this: There would be no other federal taxes and, when you die, your heirs receive what you leave them because you have already paid the tax on your money.

There should be no corporate tax because that is really a hidden tax on consumers. But as soon as someone takes a dollar of profit from a corporation it should go directly onto that person's tax return so they pay taxes on all their income by the same rules as everybody else. If a company executive or other employee takes a benefit from a corporation without claiming it as income, they should be prosecuted for tax evasion. If we still want behavior modification taxes, like gas or tobacco taxes, they should be levied by the states. No more hidden taxes, no more hidden loopholes.

Congress and the powerful financial and industrial interests who are contributing billions of dollars to them do not want a tax code that people can understand. Their claim that simplifying the tax code would result in tax cuts for the rich is a lie designed to keep us from finding out who really pays. At this point it should be clear that they can't be trusted.

In 2009 Congress is trying to add another layer of complexity to the tax code while implementing a new tax increase with a Climate Control Bill. Its mode of affecting our behavior is that we will pay this tax based on how much energy it took to produce the things we buy. Eighty five percent of the revenue produced by the tax had already been allocated to the special interests of each member of Congress who agreed to vote for it, so it has little effect on the rest of our tax liability. It does, however, put an additional burden on domestic industry which will slow our already ailing economy and push more manufacturing overseas.

The net result will be a decrease in federal tax revenue and a huge profit for the Wall Street banks that will be trading carbon credits on commission; banks like Goldman Sacs who not coincidentally gave Barack Obama over a million dollars for his 2008 campaign. It also punishes domestic energy suppliers at a time when our use of foreign oil is aiding and abetting our enemies. It does not decrease pollution, but it does increase the cost to consumers for everything we buy.

Government deriving it's just powers from the consent of the governed only works if the governed can see what their government is doing. Our system has devolved into a Congressional/Financial/Industrial Complex that operates behind a screen of deliberately impenetrable bureaucracy. The People will never be able to exercise any control over it until the system becomes simple and transparent enough that we can see what is really going on. The government needs to stay within its budget. When the president submits and Congress passes a budget, it should look like our tax return. And it should be within the amount of income generated by the paying side of our returns. If they want to spend more on one item, they should have to take it off another or raise the tax rates at the same time, on the same simple form, so we can see what they are doing to us.

SOCIAL SECURITY

Spending for the three major entitlements – Medicare, Medicaid, and Social Security – will more than double in the next 40 years. At

Dan Fragoules

that rate, entitlement spending will consume all federal tax revenues by 2052[4].

When the Social Security System was created, it was designed to take money out of our paychecks and save it in an interest bearing account to be paid back to us when we retire. It worked: our accounts grew into a lot of money. So Congress stole it. They figured they could get away with it by paying today's benefits with today's taxes. So right away they had to start stealing all the money coming into the system as well. In the early 1980's they figured out that in 2017 they would get caught because 77 million baby boomers would enter the system and there would not be enough money coming in to pay them. So in 1983 they passed a bill increasing payroll taxes to raise 5 trillion dollars by 2017[5], to keep the system from defaulting.

It would have worked, except they stole that too. They have disguised the huge payroll taxes by requiring employers to show their employees only half of the true tax. The Social Security and Medicare tax rate is 15.3 percent. Your payroll check stub shows only a 7.65 percent deduction because your employer adds the other half after your check was printed. The employer's half is either a hidden tax on the consumers of their product or service, or it is a hidden tax on your wages. These taxes brought in a surplus of 85 million dollars in 2008[6] alone, but by January 1, 2009, it was already gone. By stealing all this money they have left us with the liability of every Americans retirement with no money to pay it. This liability amounts to about 50 trillion dollars[6]. There's only one way a self funded system gets that far in the red: thieves.

It is past time to admit that our government can't be trusted with our money. We will have to take a loss but we must get our future contributions out of the hands of these people. Let everyone who wants out, out now. Make everyone else wait until age 70 to collect. And means test them. I know it's not fair, it's your money, but your money is gone. The least we can do now is stop them from stealing our children's money too. Getting rid of Social Security also plugs the biggest hole in our economic boat.

If you made $40,000 in 2008, you paid $413.33 per month into the system. If you invest that amount in a retirement account that earned 5.00% for 30 years you will retire with $345,430 in the bank[7]. Once again the solution is individual responsibility and free market competition. The government's proper role is to make the rules. It can mandate a minimum level of retirement savings, and regulate acceptable risk levels for that savings. It should regulate the companies that provide investment services. But it has no business, or Constitutional authority, to be in the retirement business or in any other business that can be or is being done by the private sector. The government cannot be your provider without also being your master.

We do need a system that prevents people from becoming indigent when they can no longer work. If we can get out of the Social Security debacle with our country intact, we can devise a new plan to accomplish that along the same lines as the health care voucher system that will be outlined in the next chapter. Replace the Social Security line on our tax return/federal budget with a line to finance vouchers to be used toward an approved investment. Then let the American people manage their own accounts out of reach of Congress and within guidelines as to risk levels and when it can be withdrawn.

"A government big enough to give you everything you want is big enough to take from you everything you have." - **Gerald Ford**

THE ECONOMY

Eighty years later the "experts" are still arguing over what caused the great depression. From a common sense point of view it seems obvious that Federal Reserve policy in the 1920's inflated a bubble which popped in 1929. And then both Hoover and Roosevelt exacerbated the problem by trying to prevent the necessary correction. The far from reasonable Tariff Act of 1930 may or may not have contributed to the depression, but it did give tariffs an unreasonably bad name that has lasted to this day.

Whatever caused the depression, there is little doubt about what it was: it was a self-sustaining decline in spending, production and earning. They make a circle: each depends on the other. FDR's "New Deal" not only failed to end the depression, it prolonged it and is still harming our economy today. Barack Obama's stimulus package was similarly impotent and will have similar long term ramifications. And the Federal Reserve is still inflating the money supply at whatever rate it takes to keep up with the ballooning Federal Government as if this bubble was for the first time in recorded history going to defy nature.

Those programs were supposed to get the cycle going again by replacing stagnant private sector spending with government spending. It didn't work in the 1930's and it won't work now. Indiscriminant government spending will not replace private sector spending as an economic stimulus because it does nothing to increase production, which would create jobs and in turn increase earning and then spending.

Our leaders keep perpetuating, and we keep going along with, the myth that government spending somehow creates wealth. But we all know that the government is just taking money from someone who earned it and giving it to someone who didn't. We keep putting up with it because we believe that we will be the recipient rather than the victim. In reality it is simply institutionalized looting that in the end will leave us all poor.

The cause of the next great depression is not hard to see. The U.S. economy is being overburdened by the massive amount of money being taken out of it by a corrupt government and their conspirators. The mission of Congress has been reduced to accumulating and retaining power. When the Bush administration pitched in with Medicare Part D, a Bully on the Playground war in Iraq, and a new Department of Homeland Security, the economic burden became debilitating. And now just when our situation is becoming dire, Barack Obama is accelerating the process.

This economy could have received a jump start for the short term by stimulating earning, spending, and production with a payroll tax cut, qualified low interest money, and reasonable import tariffs. But that's not what's going on. This is the deliberate remaking of our system for profit, the result of which will not be a representative republic. The world's history has proven that socialist economic systems leave the masses to toil in poverty to support a relatively small, rich, ruling class. Our history has proven that capitalism increases the wealth of the entire country.

In 1791 Alexander Hamilton said "Not only the wealth, but the independence and security of a country, appear to be materially connected with the prosperity of manufactures". Hamilton was as instrumental to the formation of our political and economic system as any other single person. He was at Washington's side during the revolutionary war, was instrumental in the convening of a Constitutional convention, and wrote most of the Federalist Papers which supported its ratification by the States. Then as our first Treasury Secretary, he engineered the most successful economic system in human history, the foundation of which was manufacturing. He placed tariffs on imported goods to encourage the domestic production that is still materially connected to the wealth, independence and security of this country.

Dan Fragoules

In 1981 Ronald Reagan said "the government is not the solution, the government is the problem". He knew that governments grow continuously absent any restraint and he steered us out of a recession merely by reining in its growth. It was not a stimulus package that got the economy moving again, it was the American people set free to make a profit. Reagan was elected to the White House when the cold war was at its height and our economy had suffered 10 years of inflation and slow growth. When he left office 8 years later we had created almost 30 million jobs and the Soviet Union was gone. His policies lead to the largest peacetime economic expansion in American history. And even with a lower tax rate those 30 million jobs doubled the government's revenue over the 8 years of his presidency.

Reagan's economic plan was effective because it relied on many of the same principles that worked for Hamilton. We can learn from history and still move forward. In fact, that is the only way forward. Unfortunately, Reagan failed to cut spending so his economic expansion only fed the parasite. As incomes, profits and tax revenues increased, so did Congress's appetite, which led to the inevitable slowdown that left us with a big fat hungry government that didn't have enough to eat. And we are its only source of sustenance.

The Declaration of Independence and the Constitution were crafted from the mistakes made by previous governments and include the mechanism for us to make adjustments as we learn from our own mistakes. Countries don't collapse because of forces beyond the control of their governments, and wars, depressions and recessions aren't random accidents. Our economic system is failing because of the decisions made by our leaders. It's time for We The People to make an adjustment and I don't mean switching from Democrat to Republican or visa-versa.

The size of our government has expanded steadily for the last sixty years, in part, because it is too easy to start a new program, department, or agency, and observably impossible to stop one. And it is not expanding in a vacuum; it is displacing the private sector as it grows, like a parasite feeding on its host until it kills its own food source and dies of starvation. Every day the number of people who depend on the government for income increases while fewer people are left to pay for it. We have to quit pretending that this is going to work.

Hamilton's understanding of the value of manufacturing shaped the system that gave the United States the resources to grow into a world power. If we would have had Free Trade back then, this country would not have survived past the Madison administration. Today, Free Trade policies pushed by politicians from both political parties are in the process of equalizing our standard of living with the rest of the world. Multinational corporations who profit from Free Trade have paid lawmakers and lobbyist hundreds of millions of dollars to promote their ability to move manufacturing to other countries for cheap labor and then sell their products in this country without paying a penalty. While at the same time unions are paying hundreds of millions of dollars for legislation designed to profit unions at the expense of both employers and employees in this country. The top ten donors, which include five unions, Goldman Sachs, AT&T, and the National Education Association, paid federal candidates over 300 million dollars over the last 20 years[1]. The "buy American" clause in Barack Obama's so-called stimulus package brought complaints of protectionism from economists, foreign governments, and big business. That by itself is a good argument for Buy American legislation.

From 2001 to 2008, the trade deficit increased by $350 billion a year and we lost 3.9 million Manufacturing jobs[2] because the ability of industry, particularly small business, to show a profit is being impaired by the tax system, a soup of ineffective government agencies, a corrupt legal system, unions, and Free Trade agreements that put foreign workers who pay no U. S. taxes in direct competition with American workers who do.

Unions helped build the solid manufacturing base that the wealth, independence, and security of our nation depend on. As recently as fifty or sixty years ago, when a coal miner was killed on the job his family could expect to be allowed to remain in their company owned home for two weeks before being evicted to make room for his replacement. This was the extent of the company's responsibility for the death of their employee. Unions were responsible for improving the near third world conditions that existed in many U.S. factories not all that long ago. But over the last twenty years unions have negotiated most of their member's right out of a job. It did not benefit the auto worker to insist on wages and benefits that cost his employer market share.

In the late 1980's I watched the struggle between the International Brotherhood of Electrical Workers (IBEW) and the management of the Zenith plant in Springfield, Missouri. The union had made wage concessions. But, as the last American-owned television manufacturer, all of Zenith's competition was imports. It was easy to see that if Zenith was to survive in Springfield, labor cost would have to come down. The union would not budge and Zenith moved its manufacturing to Mexico.

There were thousands of people in Springfield for whom the lower wage offered by Zenith would still have been a move up. Most of the former Zenith employees ended up taking jobs making less than the company had offered. The union hurt itself, its members and the community. The employees and management of Zenith had common interests; they had a common enemy and a common goal. The IBEW betrayed the interests of its members by dividing the very people who needed to be working together. Their common goal should have been to do whatever it took to keep Zenith in Springfield, and then work with the company to convince Congress to impose reasonable tariffs on imported TV's. Reasonable is the key word here, our trading partners need our market more than we need theirs. They will whine, but in the end they will swallow the small tariffs it would take to pay for our higher standard of living.

The problem with a big centralized government is that there is no escape from poor policy. If we followed the Constitutional system of individual, sovereign states, competition among the states would weed out bad ideas. Forty years ago states with strong unions out performed states without unions. But when unions bought national influence, they bypassed the states' rights that would have checked them before their membership, their employers, and their own organizations became so uncompetitive that we all lost.

In order to have an economy that creates jobs, we have to have an environment where companies can succeed. To start or expand a business, someone has to invest, and risk, capital. If the likelihood of profiting from that investment is not restored, there will be no new jobs. Foreign made goods come into this country tax free. Goods made in the United States carry in their price all the taxes paid by U.S. companies. If we want American workers to have unemployment insurance, workman's compensation insurance, Social Security, and Medicare, health insurance, a pension, a decent wage, and paid vacations, we cannot allow foreign manufacturers free access to our markets. The globalist and corporate Congressional financiers will disparage this as protectionism, well if a trade policy that is in the interest of the American people is protectionism, so be it.

The term "Free Trade" implies that it works both ways. I buy materials that are made in Canada and I sell my products to customers in Canada, and I can tell you that it is not free trade in both directions. The politicians who negotiated that deal were supposed to be looking out for us. They were instead repaying contributors and advancing their own global agenda. They think they are saving the poor people of the world, which is a fine idea, but that's not their job. Their job is to represent us, the fate of world's poor people have no place in the decisions being made in Congress and anyone who thinks it does should help the world's poor with their own money and get their hands out of my pocket.

A reasonable across the board tariff on imported manufactured goods will help salvage what's left of our ability to produce domestic product, and to preserve a standard of living for Americans that is higher than that of the rest of the world.

There is a lot of talk among politicians about investing in 21st Century jobs and Green jobs and that the old manufacturing jobs are a thing of the past. Well, if we quit making stuff, there will be no jobs. Manufacturing doesn't just create products, it creates demand for raw materials and it creates demand for restaurants, banks, insurance, shipping and homebuilding. It is the foundation of the economy, it's a source of opportunity for Americans who have the skill and talent to make things rather than sit behind a desk, and it is the source of almost every innovation that makes modern life better than that of every human who lived before us.

Without manufacturing there will be no middle class, no opportunity for poor people to improve their lives and no stepping stone for anybody to become wealthy. Its loss will lead to the collapse of the US economy and the bankruptcy of the United States government. The only way to survive that is to have stockpiled food and guns.

There are too many people on this planet for us to allow our economic system to fail. All of the advancements in medicine, food production, and environmental protection are made by prosperous people. Nothing that advances the planet or its people is created in poor countries. The U.S. is 5 percent of the world's population and consumes 25 percent of the world's energy[3]. But China produces more pollution every 15 days than we do in a year[4]. Protecting our economic prosperity will create the technology that will lead to a better world.

At any time in the last 50 years a collapse of the U.S. economy would have brought down the world's economy. But after the scare in 2008 and 2009 a few countries like China, Japan, and India are stealing their economies against a U.S. a failure. In a few years, the rest of the world will no longer have an interest in our survival.

Government Bail Outs

In a strictly free market banking system interest rates would be controlled by supply and demand. If more people wanted to borrow than wanted to save, rates would go up to incentivize deposits and discourage borrowing. The Federal Reserve's role is to increase the amount of money that is available for lending so that deposits can be available for both lending and withdrawal. The flaw in this plan as it is being practiced today is that there is no gold, or anything else behind our money. Every dollar the Fed injects into the economy with one hand it is taking out of our pockets with the other.

Banks don't make anything, grow anything or dig anything up. The only thing that supports them is people who do. Government policies, our legal system, and the influence of unions and other special interest groups reduced the manufacturing segment of our economy to less than 12% of GDP by 2008[5], at the same time the financial sectors share of the economy was growing. The system became top-heavy and collapsed. The financial geniuses in our government think that adding another two trillion dollars to the Federal Deficit to prop up these failed investment banks and insurance companies will help our economy. The truth is they know better, they're just protecting their own interest at the expense of the American people.

There are thousands of healthy banks in this country who provide honest service to their customers. If our monetary policy was designed to make money available to those banks so they could loan it to people to start and expand businesses and to the consumers who purchase their products, the economy would thrive. Those businesses and consumers are the economy; without them, all the banks in the world are worthless. Any bank that does not loan money to the enterprise segment of our economy is worthless, including these big multinational investment banks that make money trading invented instruments and manufactured securities. They are called toxic assets because they are not worth what the banks pretend they are.

Obama, Geitner, and Congress are using our money to put the corrupt banks and the US government in competition with the banks in your community who have played by the rules. And they are doing it because the big banks are paying them. In 2009, while Congress was pretending to be outraged by AIG bonuses, they were still taking millions of dollars from AIG. They passed the law allowing the bonuses at the same time they gave AIG the public money to pay the bonuses with. They knew what they were doing, they are arrogant and they think they are so much smarter than the rest of us that we will put up with it. Sadly, that's just what we did.

These banks gambled and spent their companies into bankruptcy while company executives took bonuses of 180 billion dollars during the 8 years of George W. Bush's Presidency, 33 billion in 2007 alone[6]. And they spent millions of dollars lobbying the government officials who were suppose to be regulating them. They victimized the American people with millions of credit card offers designed to trick consumers into contracts that look good on the surface, but left them paying default rates of 20 and 30 percent. Then Congress, George W. Bush, Barack Obama, Hank Paulson and Tim Geitner used our money to bail out their companies.

I have worked in the marine industry for thirty years. My business depends on the sale of new boats for much of its revenue. Those sales were down thirty percent in 2008 and another 20 percent in 2009. The single largest contributing factor in the fifty percent drop over a two year period was the lack of available credit. Boat manufacturers depend on dealer orders, dealers need financing to buy inventory, and their customers need financing to buy boats. This industry, along with the rest of the economy cannot survive without a healthy banking system. In order to have that, we have to get rid of corrupt banks that are "too big to fail", not bail them out.

The Collapse of the Housing Market

Incentive makes house payments. If you have twenty thousand dollars invested in your home, you will spend your weekends improving it and you will take a second job to keep it. But what if you're poor? Don't you have as much right to own a home as I do? The answer is no. Our Constitution ensures that you have a right to the same opportunity to own a home as I do.

In another example of our government overstepping its legal authority, Congress mandated that home loans be given to millions of Americans with no down payment. Even taxes and insurance were often rolled into the mortgage. They did this on such a large scale, nearly half the mortgages in the whole country, that it caused a building boom and inflated home values, which lead to home equity loans. When high oil prices sparked a slowdown in our economy, a relatively small number of very big banks found that a substantial amount of their assets were over-valued homes in which the mortgage holders had no investment. When the mortgage holders saw that their homes were worth less than they owed, it was easy to quit making the house payment in favor of buying gas and food. There is no incentive here to take a second job to keep the house.

This was another result of a big central government. If a larger number of smaller banks would have loaned out the same amount of money, the economic slowdown would have weeded out the high risk lenders while leaving the healthy banks in place.

Fannie Mae and Freddie Mac initiated and supported this scheme when they guaranteed the individual loans that no bank would have made otherwise, and then purchased millions of subprime mortgages, thereby creating a market for them. 354 members of Congress took 10 million dollars from these two companies[1], which by 2008 held 5.3 trillion dollars worth of mortgages in the US.

Members of Congress took $72 million dollars from AIG, which also, through the CEO's foundation, gave $25 million dollars to other PACs and lobbyist. Goldman Sachs investment banking firm and its employees have spent more than $43 million dollars on lobbying and campaign contributions[1]. The executives of these companies along with most of the United States Congress ran this scheme for profit and we were their mark.

If Congress would have stayed out of it, many of the people that Freddy and Fannie "helped" would have saved, ask for help from parents, and given up their second car to come up with a down payment to buy a home. The only people the government helped were the handful of banks, which with their connections in Congress became so big that their failure would threaten the whole system. It's simple, if you can't afford a house; it's a bad idea to buy it. The government's involvement in this industry damaged the housing market, the banking industry, and the economy. The reason they were involved was because they were accepting bribes to do so.

There is no easy way out of this. Fannie, Freddy and the Wall Street banks took trillions of dollars and we took the loss. As with the rest of the banking crisis, the only way the government can help is for the Federal Reserve to make low interest money available to the thousands of honest, healthy banks in this country on terms that would allow them to provide long term fixed rate mortgages to qualified borrowers. This would accomplish more than the TARP plan and the stimulus package combined and yet cost much less. The only thing it doesn't do is pay back political favors and enrich crooked members of Congress. The key word though is "qualified borrowers". The collapse of the housing market and the banking crisis wasn't caused by too much credit and too much debt; it was caused by indiscriminate credit and unreliable debt.

While a responsible Federal Reserve could have helped our economy through this crisis it is important to note that the Federal Reserve is anything but responsible. No American's wealth is safe as long as the Fed can print billions of paper dollars, backed by absolutely nothing, and with absolutely no oversight. They should back up deposits and facilitate lending with money from the U.S.

Treasury which would require just enough responsible behavior from congress to not spend every dime they collect.

The printing must stop, it is not only a hidden tax, it enables excess government spending and is destabilizing our economy. The amount of money in the system must be constant in order for its value to be stable. That's why it used to be backed by gold, because there is a finite amount of gold. Now the dollar is backed only by the honor of the Federal Reserve. Unfortunately that's not a commodity whose value is increased by its scarcity.

The US Auto Industry

What got these companies in trouble was not building bad cars. It was not that they didn't build small efficient cars. They built good cars of the size and kind that we wanted to buy. Their problem was a management system that paid too many people who were not building cars, a United Auto Workers Union (UAW) who couldn't see the goose for the golden egg, a legal system that follows money rather than justice, a tax system that punishes the reinvestment of profits, hundreds of government agencies with millions of ever changing rules and regulations, and our government's policy of letting foreign manufacturers who don't pay workers compensation insurance, unemployment insurance, healthcare, or U.S. taxes compete for free. Then the people who run these companies thought it was appropriate to continue the multi-million dollar executive packages, high management salaries and $73.00 per hour employee packages[8] while they ask the rest of us who make an average of $28.50 per hour[9] to bail them out.

A ditch digger would have known that losing three or four thousand dollars every time you build a vehicle to support these excesses was going to lead to bankruptcy. But GM's management, the UAW, and the Federal Government they were in bed with did not see it coming. I'm not disparaging ditch diggers; I'm just saying that maybe the stockholders of GM should have hired one.

There were 355,000 Americans directly employed by the big three auto makers. One out of every ten jobs in America was in some way dependant on these three companies. The loss of those jobs will domino through our economy, unemployment will skyrocket, and government revenues will plummet. Bailing out these companies seemed cheap by comparison, but it will really just compound the problem. Many people died for our right to be free, it's not our place to trade it for a few million jobs.

With liberty comes responsibility; you can't have one without the other and GM's management, the UAW, and even their employees need to pay the consequences of failure. They took the money when they were profitable, and kept taking it long after they started losing money. The UAW took salaries that were three times what the average American makes for three decades while their competitors steadily took their market share. The only interest the government has any business considering in this matter is the American taxpayer.

Unfortunately that won't happen because the UAW ranks 16th in money given to federal candidates[10] and the U.S auto industry ranks 34th [1]. What the government needs to do is reform the bankruptcy system so that failed companies like GM and Chrysler can be restructured or sold quickly and without losing assets to attorney's fees.

Instead, they borrowed $56 billion dollars[11], on behalf of the taxpayers, and gave it to General Motors and Chrysler. That would have been enough money to loan a million dollars each to 56 thousand small businesses. If those one out of every ten jobs in America were dependant on several hundred smaller car companies instead of three giant ones, this would be a much more stable, innovative and competitive industry. The fact that so much of our economy was dependant on just three big companies is a serious flaw in the system. This flaw is a direct result of the fact that Congressional representation is for sale and small companies can't afford it.

The void left by the failure of GM and Chrysler should have been filled by new, healthy, smaller and more numerous car companies. They would have been innovative, competitive, and the rest of the world would have once again had to catch up with US. The wealth, independence and security of our nation depend on it.

Healthcare

Our health care system is in desperate need of reform. But this President and this Congress do not intend to reform anything, anymore than the last one did. They're not going to reform Medicare, Medicaid, the VA or HHS. Instead, they're going to add new government programs, another layer of bureaucracy and spend more money. Any reform that doesn't replace those programs will fail. Any system that pays for all of our health care will fail because we won't care how much it cost. Any system that doesn't require discipline from everyone involved will fail. And any plan that is designed by a Congress who is taking money from the corporations involved will fail. Part of the problem is that the health insurance industry is paying Congress millions of dollars to get the rules made in their favor. And the more involved the government gets, the more they have for sale. That's why campaign contributions and federal spending increase at a similar pace.

This could be fixed if we just use some common sense. First define what we should reasonably expect from a health care system: that everyone has a provider, that your provider does a good job, that you can afford it, that the treatments and technology improve over time, and that the cost of a catastrophic illness is covered by insurance. Then design a system that replaces the failing programs currently in place with a plan that creates the incentives that will encourage everyone involved, the providers, patients, insurance companies and the government, to behave in a manner that will bring it about.

So far the government's involvement has made health care unaffordable to everyone outside its programs and most who are in their programs receive less than the best care. Over 60 percent of the personal bankruptcies filed in this country are caused by major medical expenses even though three quarters of them have insurance[12], and most of our health care dollars are spent treating preventable conditions. Under our current system, when a serious illness or injury prevents you from going to work, your premiums get harder, usually impossible, to pay and the insurance company cancels your policy.

Even if you can keep paying the premiums, the co-pays and deductibles will force you into bankruptcy, so the public pays the bill in higher health care cost, insurance cost and taxes. Since this puts the wealth and property of the American people at risk, and since the government is already involved to such a degree that they are responsible for most of the problems, they are going to have to be involved in the solution. But they do not have the legal authority to participate in the business of health care or health insurance.

The solution is simple: shut down Medicare, Medicaid, and every other government involvement, including veteran, Indian, and government employee health care, and replace it with a system where taxpayers contribute to major medical expenses in the form of vouchers used toward the purchase of private, major medical insurance that will cover ninety seven percent of everything after the first two thousand dollars each year. The taxpayer's liability would be the same for a tobacco using alcoholic as for someone with a healthy life style so personal responsibility will determine to what extent you will have to supplement the voucher with your own money.

Every American should be eligible for a voucher if they are a legal resident, can pass a drug test, and is not delinquent on any taxes, child support, or other court ordered debts. If you want to buy insurance for the first two thousand dollars, it will be cheap because the insurance company's liability will be limited. If you're worried about the poor, the unemployed and children, donate your time or money to a charity to help them. That will be cheap too for the same reason. Then rest easy knowing that under this plan the poorest American will treated just like a U.S. senator.

We are retrieving our freedom, we are going to take care of ourselves, and we are going to take responsibility for our own choices.

The only people who can control cost and police the quality of health care are the American people spending our own money. If you are not paying for it, you have no control over it. If you're not paying for it, providers have no reason to care whether you like it. In a healthy, private sector health care system, competing health care providers would provide checkups and screenings because taking care of your customer is good business. The government should provide guidelines as to which tests should be performed at what age to detect preventable conditions, but it cannot take over our responsibility to take care of ourselves. If you eat healthy food and exercise you shouldn't be forced to pay the medical bills of someone who spends twelve hours a day in a recliner eating chips, not in America.

Routine medical expenses would be manageable in a free market system that was not corrupted by government involvement. The competition will actually make it cheaper, better, and encourage service innovations in preventative care that will further reduce costs. We could all decide for ourselves what lifestyle risk to take, and what kind of healthcare to purchase, without adding to everyone else's cost. If you don't have to worry about losing your home to a major accident or illness, and you don't have to pay for everyone else's poor choices, you will be able to afford your own care. The only exception would be anyone needing care related to military service; they should receive a check from the Defense Department equal to all their co-pays. Everyone else needs to take responsibility for themselves. If we want to be free, we have to stop asking the government to do for us the things we should do for ourselves.

The major medical voucher system will cost less than we now spend on Medicare, Medicaid and veteran, active military and federal employee health care. It should be financed with one line on a simplified tax return so that each taxpayer knows exactly what it cost. If you made forty thousand dollars in 2008, you paid $1054.56 into the Medicare system, half of it is shown on your pay stub as a deduction and by law half of it hidden from you. And if you are under 65, you received nothing in return. In 2008, I paid just under $1000.00 for an Arkansas Blue Cross Blue Shield major medical insurance policy. So much of the cost of this system will be offset just by eliminating Medicare. The elimination of all other government health care programs will offset the rest and then some.

Every American should have access to the same health care, you should expect your provider to do a good job, and you should be able to afford it. Your health care provider should take an active role in notifying and encouraging you to receive the preventative care that will ultimately reduce your health care cost. This plan will save the best health care system in the world.

The only place in the world where new drugs are developed is the United States, because this is the only place where the profit potential gives the pharmaceutical companies the incentive to invest in the research. There is a reason we have the best health care in the world: free enterprise. If the government takes medicine out of the private sector there will be no new drugs, no new medical equipment and the brightest people will go into other fields.

The government has a role to play, but it can't give you health care. It would work the same as when the government tried to give everyone a house. It will be just like Social Security, the Post Office, and Amtrak. It will cost more and be worth less. It will kill research and innovation. Medical advancement will stop here. The private sector can do this if the government supports a system that provides incentives that encourage it. We will never have a workable health care system if we don't control cost. It is proven every day in a thousand agencies that the government cannot control cost. Only market forces can do it. When a hurricane or ice storm destroys a community, it is not FEMA who shows up the next day with generators and food, it is Lowes, Home Depot and Wal-Mart.

Like banks, insurance companies have to be regulated because they are entrusted with other people's money. That is the government's role. It is not to be an insurance company, it's to make the rules insurance companies and health care providers must follow. One of those rules should be that if you sell a drug or provide a service for an insurance company for one price you have to give everyone else the same price. My last Blue Cross Blue Shield statement showed a bill from a doctor for $469.00. But, it stated, your provider has agreed to accept what Blue Cross Blue Shield allows for this procedure, $114.00. That means if you have this insurance they will do it for $114.00 but if you pay cash they get $469.00.

And like lawyers, doctors need to be regulated by non doctors. Each state's Governor should appoint a board that is not made up entirely of doctors or lawyers to hear complaints and discipline doctors. They should actually remove bad doctors, unlike the current tort system which punishes good and bad doctors for profit and disciplines none of them.

Education

The corruption in our government affects every aspect of our society, but education is probably the most susceptible because the citizens in this case are children. The centralized control of our educational system has systematically weeded out any innovation or competition, while at the same time, the "by, for, and of" the money way we run the Federal Government has left the children completely unrepresented. The crafting of education policy brings as much money into the pockets of the 552 decision makers as any other subject, none of it from children and very little of it from their parents. As a result, the taxpayers borrowed over 67 billion dollars in 2008 and more than 140 billion in 2009[1], and spent it at the direction of teachers unions and big corporations.

An efficient and effective education system is vital to long term economic stability but that is not a result we can expect from this process. We need to take control away from the government and give it to parents. If we want to use the Federal Government's power to tax as an equalizer in the system, it should be done by using the education line on our tax return/federal budget to finance vouchers that parents can use to purchase education from state regulated providers.

Most teachers are dedicated to their students and they deserve to be part of a system that provides the best possible results and that rewards higher performing educators and punishes poor performance.

> *"Politics is supposed to be the second oldest profession. I have*
> *come to realize that it bears a very close resemblance to the first."*
> **- Ronald Reagan.**

ENERGY, FOREIGN POLICY, AND IMMIGRATION

According to the Department of Defense the United States military has more than 600,000 individual buildings at more than 6,000 locations, on more than 30 million acres in 135 countries:

> Afghanistan, Albania, Algeria, Antigua, Argentina, Australia, Austria, Azerbaijan, Bahamas, Bahrain, Bangladesh, Barbados, Belgium, Belize, Bolivia, Bosnia and Herzegovina, Botswana, Brazil, Bulgaria, Burma, Burundi, Cambodia, Cameroon, Canada, Chad, Chile, China, Colombia, Congo, Costa Rica, Cote D'lvoire, Cuba, Cyprus, Czech Republic, Denmark, Djibouti, Dominican Republic, East Timor, Ecuador, Egypt, El Salvador, Eritrea, Estonia, Ethiopia, Fiji, Finland, France, Georgia, Germany, Ghana, Greece, Guatemala, Guinea, Haiti, Honduras, Hungary, Iceland, India, Indonesia, Iraq, Ireland, Israel, Italy, Jamaica, Japan, Jordan, Kazakhstan, Kenya, Kuwait, Kyrgyzstan, Laos, Latvia, Lebanon, Liberia, Lithuania, Luxembourg, Macedonia, Madagascar, Malawi, Malaysia, Mali, Malta, Mexico, Mongolia, Morocco, Mozambique, Nepal, Netherlands, New Zealand, Nicaragua, Niger, Nigeria, North Korea, Norway, Oman, Pakistan, Paraguay, Peru, Philippines, Poland, Portugal, Qatar, Romania, Russia, Saudi Arabia, Senegal, Serbia and Montenegro, Sierra Leone, Singapore, Slovenia, Spain, South Africa, South Korea, Sri Lanka, Suriname, Sweden, Switzerland, Syria,

Tanzania, Thailand, Togo, Trinidad and Tobago, Tunisia, Turkey, Turkmenistan, Uganda, Ukraine, United Arab Emirates, United Kingdom, Uruguay, Venezuela, Vietnam, Yemen, Zambia, and Zimbabwe.

We need a military presence in the world, but having troops in all these countries does not serve the interests of the American people. It serves the interest of corrupt politicians who are using our money to increase their wealth and power. Defense contractors gave over 23 million dollars to federal candidates in both parties in 2008 alone[1]. Other multinational corporations with business interests in many of these countries gave millions more to the same members of Congress who appropriate our money to the defense budget. And they all gave millions of dollars to Bill Clinton, George W. Bush and Barack Obama.

There is only one country that our troops should be defending and that is the United States of America. They should stop every illegal entry into this country. There are twenty thousand nuclear warheads in the world belonging to 9 countries including North Korea, Pakistan, India and China. Within a few years Iran, Libya and Syria will have nuclear weapons. The number of individuals who have or could have access to any of these weapons is impossible to tell. But whatever the number, if we don't control our borders, eventually we will lose a city.

The 552 people who run the Federal Government each took an oath to defend the Constitution. They have an obligation to protect this country yet they are allowing millions of people to enter it illegally. Three of the 9/11 pilots were illegal aliens. According to Homeland Security, from 2001 to 2005 45,008 illegal aliens from countries on the U.S. list of state-sponsors of terror or from countries that protected terrorist organizations and their members, were caught entering the US illegally and were then released into the general population.

Every day in the United States, illegal aliens murder 12 Americans, kill 13 more Americans while driving drunk and rape 8 American children[2]. It is one thing to sacrifice our freedom and our children's freedom by spending all that two or three generations can repay, but this is something else. The third world population on this planet grows by 100 million people every 18 months. There are over 15 million people in this country illegally and they are coming here at an escalating rate of over a half a million people each year[3]. It doesn't take a genius to tell how this story will end.

When George W. Bush used 9/11 as an excuse to shift more power to the Federal Government, we should have asked him this question: If we need the Department of Homeland Security to protect the homeland, what do we need the Department of Defense for? It is time for the United States of America to defend the United States of America. And it's time for the rest of the world to defend their own borders, fight their own wars and pay their own bills!

If there were no oil in Iraq, we would not have gone to war there. It is not that we went to war to get the oil or even to protect it. We went to war because the value of the oil in Iraq is a source of political and financial power. We spent thousands of lives and a trillion dollars without asking if we could afford it, how we were going to pay for it and if what we gained would be worth the cost. Nor did we ask the more important question: Was it in the interest of the American people to invade Iraq?

Our government created fictitious intelligence to justify sending troops to Viet Nam, and even knowing how that turned out, we did the same thing to send troops to Iraq. If our government was required to balance its budget, they would have had to debate what they would give up to pay for the invasion. That may have lead to the consideration of alternatives. If instead of invading Iraq, we would have switched the nation's trucks, buses and government vehicles from diesel to natural gas, we could have reduced the value of Iraq's oil, effectively neutralizing any threat they posed to this country.

At the same time this would have diverted the 18 billion dollars a month that we spend on imported oil to the US economy. This is an important security consideration because our country is not now fiscally strong enough to withstand another 9/11 style terrorist attack. The most important weapon we have is our economic strength, which we are squandering in part by interfering with the internal politics of foreign countries.

Ronald Reagan became the leader of the Free World with no experience in foreign policy. He faced an aggressively expanding evil empire that had not lost a communist country to the west since WORLD WAR II. He brought down that empire with intellectual gamesmanship that included decisions that helped shape the world we live in today. Before the Soviet Union went to war in Afghanistan, India, Pakistan, and Afghanistan were not military threats to the United States. During that war, the United States covertly supported Afghanistan in an effort to hurt the Soviets. That effort was successful and contributed to the fall of that empire. However, in order to accomplish that we brought Afghanistan into the modern age militarily. Our involvement in that part of the world both before and during the 1980s helped Pakistan and India become nuclear powers.

The defeat of the Soviet Union came at a price that few people doubt was worth it. But we cannot ignore the lesson of the consequences of interfering in the military strength of other countries. For years we provided military resources to the government of Iran. Without our help Iran would not be a world power. We provided military aid to revolutionary forces in Iraq, helping to bring Saddam Hussein to power. The CIA supplied arms and intelligence to both sides of the Iran-Iraq war. More often than not, when we give military technology to another country they eventually shoot it back at us. After WORLD WAR II, we assassinated foreign leaders, overthrew elected governments and financed wars in dozens of countries. We have spent billions of dollars and thousands of lives trying to change the world, only to have made it a more dangerous place.

The United States was the most fertile ground in human history for liberty to take root and it still took most of 200 years to build a republic of free citizens. We can foster Democracy around the world, but only by example and with the exportation of technology. It cannot be done by force and in most countries representative governments would not work at all. Successful representative governments require a prosperous electorate. If you give the vote to a nation of desperate or impoverished people they will bring their government down out of necessity. We are five percent of the population of the world. We cannot save the other ninety five percent unless we are strong and free. As it is, we will be lucky if we save our own Republic.

Since World War II, the CIA has provided inaccurate information to eleven presidents. They have assassinated elected leaders and overthrown elected governments. They were duped by China during the Korean War, by the Soviets during the cold war, and by Castro for most of the last fifty years. They have provided weapons and military support to both sides of wars all over the world and have even supported people that the U.S. military had to fight. I believe that the CIA's mission could be better accomplished by other branches of military intelligence. It might be that in a free and open society we are more effective when we say what we mean, out loud, and do what we say.

There are some things that our government has proven it can do better than anyone in the world, like space travel and satellite navigation. And at the top of that list are the Army, Navy, Air Force and Marines. It is because of hard work, discipline, and honor. They depend on each other for their lives and they are not afraid to risk their lives for our country. We need to gather intelligence and it needs to be complete, accurate and get to the President and others who need it. That was supposed to be the CIA's job, a job that they have failed to perform. Within two years of its start in 1980, CNN had a far more extensive, faster, and more accurate, information gathering organization than the CIA did after more than 60 years and billions of dollars. How long does something have to not work before we stop doing it?

Today we face a world where Islamic extremists want to bring down our nation and our way of life. Like the cold war this is a war of ideas. We will only win if we stay ahead technologically, restore our manufacturing capabilities, restore our financial viability by making our government fiscally responsible, and quit financing our enemies by buying their oil. Our Foreign Policy should be shaped by which countries are a threat to the safety and security of America. How we deal with our energy needs will determine how well financed some of those countries are. And how strong our economy is will determine how well financed we are.

We can replace foreign oil with domestic natural gas practically overnight. The goal of Al Gore's Repower America is right in the long run, but we can't afford his methods. He would eliminate coal fired power plants and double the cost of electricity to accelerate the transition to alternative fuels. Much of the alternative energy/global warming movement does not support the conversion to natural gas because they think it would slow the transition to wind and solar. Wind and solar will be the energy of the future. But if we continue to import 400 million barrels of oil every month, we may not have a future.

Natural gas and even "clean" coal will allow us to get off of foreign oil during the transition to alternative sources. This may slow that transition, but staying on oil to speed up the process is not worth the cost. We need a bridge fuel that will get us off of foreign oil while we develop the technology for wind and solar. Sending 18 billion dollars a month to the Middle East is making that part of the world very dangerous. Diverting that money to our domestic sources would help to rescue our economy.

We have a huge domestic supply of energy that burns cleaner and cost less than foreign oil. We are not using it because the oil industry pays members of Congress millions of dollars each year and as of 2009 the natural gas industry has not.

Immigration

Energy, national defense and immigration are so interconnected that any attempt to solve one must include a solution to all three. The one constant in all of the problems facing our country is that they all have the same root cause, that the representative nature of our government has been perverted by money.

It is a fact of life that capital, goods and people are moving freely across our borders. And that this is the conscious goal of our government in spite of the fact that a majority of the people they pretend to represent do not support this policy. Why does U.S. immigration policy ignore the obvious national defense considerations and the wishes of the American people? Because the multi-national corporations, who profit from our dependence on oil and free trade, are paying people in our government. Most of the oil we import comes from Mexico and Canada. This doesn't change the fact that every dollar we spend on oil supports our enemies in the rest of the world but it does make any control of our borders difficult if we don't address the energy question at the same time.

If we continue on our current path, the softening of our borders will continue until they disappear. The integration of the United States, Canada and Mexico into a North American Union tied together by superhighways and railroads is not just a figment of the imagination of a few paranoid radicals; it is the inevitable result of our current policy. For whatever reason, our government is purposely trading our island of freedom for a piece of the new world order.

THE THIRD BRANCH

Law is an honorable profession. Some of our greatest leaders were lawyers. Thomas Jefferson, Alexander Hamilton, John Adams, James Madison, Daniel Webster, Abraham Lincoln. Unfortunately this profession has been corrupted by the same thing that has corrupted other honorable institutions. It has too much power and too little oversight.

The practice of law is a business which operates for profit. There's nothing wrong with that; but there is something wrong with that business controlling an entire branch of the government and operating it for profit. It is the only trade that entirely regulates and disciplines itself. Bar Associations are supposedly there to discipline lawyers, but instead they enable corrupt behavior on both sides of the bench. Attorneys are the only professionals not protected by whistleblower laws. To the contrary, in many cases it is disbarable offense for an attorney to publicly criticize another attorney or judge, or for judges to criticize each other. Of the hundreds of thousands of complaints filed with bar association disciplinary commissions each year, few results in discipline and some result in legal threats against whoever filed the complaint.

There are three sides to every law suit: the plaintiff's lawyer, the defendant's lawyer and the judge. And there are three winners in every law suit: the plaintiff's lawyer, the defendant's lawyer and the judge. For every judge to be a lawyer makes about as much since as for every traffic cop to be a speeder. Lawyers need oversight that cannot be provided by another lawyer.

The U.S. economy depends on small business for most of its jobs and several of the most serious challenges facing small business in the

United States today are caused by abuses in the legal system. When a business is successful, its employees spend their earnings, supporting other jobs. When a company fails, everyone who worked for that company loses their job, and all the places that used to benefit from their spending suffer also.

Another result of a company's failure is that its assets fall under the control of a bankruptcy judge, who appoints a trustee, another lawyer, to oversee the liquidation and distribution of those assets. The trustee hires a lawyer to represent his interest in the case and another lawyer to represent unsecured creditors and, depending on the value of the assets, a few more lawyers. The trustee then goes to work selling assets, collecting additional funds from the company's receivables, and going back and recovering money that had been recently paid out by the company to its vendors. All the while collecting attorney's fees that are paid out of the assets they are guarding. Over the next few years the lawyers will make every effort to collect all of the assets in fees. The suppliers, who have just lost a customer, now also lose all the money that was owed them, in many cases sending them into bankruptcy as well. At least the lawyers get to keep working.

We are not talking about a few isolated cases. It happens every time a company files chapter 7 Bankruptcy. One of my customers filed bankruptcy on December 1, 2004 and I was still receiving court documents authorizing the payment of attorney's fees in April of 2009, over 4 years later. While over the same period, not one dime was paid to unsecured creditors.

Any small business that survives the bankruptcy attorneys is likely to eventually be involved in a product liability suit. The plaintiff has been injured in an accident and claims that several product manufacturers are at fault, because in the business of law, guilt is where the money is. His lawyer takes the case without charging him. This "nice guy" would only collect his fee if he gets a judgment. The defendants are represented by lawyers who are paid by their product liability insurance carriers.

The plaintiff's lawyer knows the case has no merit but he knows it will cost the insurance companies twenty or thirty thousand dollars each to fight it, so he settles out of court for about 15 thousand dollars each and collects it all in attorney's fees. The defendant's lawyers collect their fees, the Judge collects his salary; a profitable venture all around, except for the companies who have to pay for product liability insurance.

In theory, the court system is there to protect our rights. In practice, it is there to create profit for lawyers. Most lawsuits are brought for no other reason than to create attorney's fees. The discovery that asbestos caused cancer prevented thousands of cancer deaths because we quit using the stuff. It also created billions of dollars in attorney's fees. More than 700,000 claims have been filed pertaining to asbestos in the last 30 years. By 2004 asbestos litigation had already bankrupted 70 corporations and cost $70 billion dollars, the total cost to our economy will exceed 300 billion, ten times what has been paid to compensate victims[1].

We have the best health care in the world, but we face a health care crisis because the cost is threatening to destroy our economy. Medical malpractice liability, the "tort tax" on doctors and hospitals, is estimated to cost the average American family of four about $4,000 a year[2]. Defensive medicine inflates health care costs by encouraging unnecessary procedures and referrals that doctors and hospitals prescribe in order to limit their exposure to future litigation. Our liability system does not efficiently deter bad conduct, it punishes indiscriminately for profit. Doctors and hospitals are not sued because they make mistakes; they are sued because they have money.

Another crisis our country faces is the insolvency of the Social Security System. Misuse of Social Security Disability is part of the problem. The legal profession, with their influence in Congress, has perverted the system from one that paid eligible disabled Americans to one that pays anyone who hires an attorney that practices Social Security Disability law. It's a good bet that everyone knows someone who collects SSD who should be working. According to the Social Security Administration, disability benefits were paid to more than 8.1 million people in 2007 at a rate of 7.8 billion dollars per month. As with most of the independent government agencies, the problem is that the government should not be operating it in the first place.

Much of the court system is being used by judges and lawyers to enrich judges and lawyers at our expense. As a victim of this system the only place to go for justice is another judge or lawyer. If you go to Congress, you find more lawyers who have taken millions of dollars from other lawyers. Lawyers are no different than bankers or Congressmen, if we allow them access to our money and expect them to police themselves, it will turn them into thieves.

Just like the executive and legislative branches of government, the judicial branch has become too powerful, too independent, and too far from the people they are supposed to represent. The governors of each state should appoint a mostly non-attorney commission to hear complaints about, and to discipline, lawyers and judges who practice in their states, including federal judges. And future nominees to the Supreme Court should be non-attorneys until at least four seats are held by non-attorneys. The states and the people must regain their Constitutional *sovereignty* over all three branches of government. It is time to separate the business of law from the third branch of government and to return honor to the practice of law.

HISTORY

"Study the past if you would divine the future." - *Confucius*

If our Republic survives it will be because people like Alexander Hamilton, Thomas Jefferson and John Adams left us with two documents whose wisdom is far greater than that of the men who wrote them. By what miracle the Declaration and Constitution came to us with all the tools we need to triumph over a renegade Congress, Islamic extremist, and an invasion of illegal immigrants, we will never know. But it does, these words will be more valuable than money or guns to the future of America.

We paid a high price for those documents. *Give me liberty or give me death* are not just words from our history. 25 thousand people died winning our independence and over a million Americans have died since, defending it. It should shame us to be consciously discarding what so many gave their lives for. And shame on us if we leave our children no choice but to fight and die to regain it.

Our forefathers took on the most powerful nation on earth against impossible odds to replace oppression and servitude with justice and liberty. For thousands of years their ancestors had lived in poverty while lords and kings lived high off of their labor. Americans even during the poverty and suffering of the great depression had something no common man had ever had before. They had the rule of law. Their daughters weren't raped or their sons killed by a ruling class who owned all the rights. Be wary of a ruling class that is above the law.

History is full of stories of battles won against great odds. In 490 BC, 10,000 Athenians defeated 50,000 Persians. In 331, BC Darius

III was defeated by Alexander's army of half its size. In 1346, Edward the III of England defeated 36,000 French soldiers with an army of 12,000. And in 1415, Henry V massacred 36,000 French soldiers at Agincourt with 8,000 sick and hungry Englishmen. The difference was leadership.

History is also full of stories of great empires that no longer exist. You don't lose battles because your soldiers aren't as good, and you don't lose countries because your people aren't strong. You lose them when you are failed by your leaders.

Too many of the people who are running our country today have studied law and economics and two few of them have studied history. Too few of our citizens in general have learned enough history to appreciate how good we have it or how close we are to losing it. The lessons of a depression and two misguided wars lasted only a generation. Most young people are not interested in history because most history teachers want them to memorize dates and names, instead of telling them the story. I'm sorry, but if you can't make the lives of Alexander Hamilton or Andrew Jackson sound interesting, then you should not be teaching history.

This country was a better place from day one. People came here from all over the world looking for a better life. America was an island of opportunity in a world of tyranny. The history of the United States is a fantastic story. We defeated the most powerful nation on the planet with a few thousand underfed and under equipped soldiers who marched hundreds of miles in winter without boots. Then we had the audacity to cross the ocean and make war against Tripoli to whom every other seafaring nation was content to pay protection money.

In 1812, England dominated the seas with hundreds of warships that had outfought the navies of the world for so long that they were no longer challenged. But with only six frigates our new navy dealt them defeat after defeat and took away the psychological advantage they had used to intimidate the entire world. When their army, the best trained army in the world, met Andrew Jackson's volunteers in the battle of New Orleans they lost over two thousand men, we lost 71.

We were better because we were free, but also because we innovated. Our warships were different than anything that had ever been built before. Our innovation came sometimes from our lack of access to Europe's resources, but it was also part of the mindset of this new world. The Europeans were doing things the same way they had for three hundred years, using the same tools, passing knowledge through the generations. Their tools would last for a hundred years. We made do with what we had, and if it didn't last we just made another one, improving the design each time. The freedom we had won here gave us the ability to reap the benefits of our successes and the responsibility to pay the price for our failures, the carrot and stick that gave us an advantage over the rest of the world.

For all that science has discovered we may be alone in the universe. This earth may be the only place that life has ever existed, and we may be the only intelligent species to have ever existed. If this is so, then the spark that is human intelligence is the brightest thing to happen in the universe since the big bang itself. And this country is the brightest thing to happen to our species since the invention of writing. This would seem to place some responsibility on us to get it right. There is something extraordinary going on here. It is an opportunity unique in all of time to move forward, to grow humanity into something better. We will all live our lives and die leaving the next generation to start where we leave off. The value of our lifetime may be measured by whether our children start their lives from a better place than we started ours. If that is true, our grandparents are in heaven and we are going to hell.

Congress has stolen our money, our freedom, and our future. And we have allowed them to do it. The men we have put in the White House since World War II, while mostly good men, have to varying degrees either helped or failed to stop them. In 1980, I thought that Ronald Reagan's election had come in the nick of time. I believed he would turn us off the course of spending the country into bankruptcy. His economic policies did buy us some time, but he was unable to bring spending under any kind of control. He also failed to control immigration, didn't get rid of the department of education or any of the other unnecessary federal agencies and departments, and went one step too far when he extended his deregulation policies to the banking industry.

He was, nonetheless, a great president. He believed in the greatness of America and its people, and he left his country in better shape than he found it. When he took office, the Soviet Union had thousands of nuclear armed missiles aimed at the United States. His strategies won the cold war and his investments in technology contributed to our success in Operation Desert Storm and made possible the subsequent cuts in defense spending that lead to the budget surpluses under the Clinton administration. His economic policies worked. He was right about where success comes from, "not the government", and nobody thought they could influence him by giving money to his campaign fund. Nobody thought that the things he fought for were politically motivated, but of course you could say the same about Jimmy Carter.

But Carter had two character flaws that made him unqualified for the office of president. He thought people were basically good. And he was a genius. Richard Nixon had totally different character flaws; he was paranoid and dishonest. These two things made him dangerous. If it wouldn't have been for Nixon, Gerald Ford would never have been president and yet, if it wasn't for Nixon, Gerald Ford could have been a great president. During his two years in office he vetoed more spending bills than any other president in history. In Reagan's fight with Congress' spending habits, he begged the American people for a line item veto. Ford just vetoed every bill that had excessive spending or earmarks. The American people liked Gerald Ford. Had it not been for his association with Nixon, Ford could have changed this country back when it wasn't too late. I just wish he would have told us who really killed President Kennedy before he died.

Since I brought it up, I want to make a point about Kennedy's assassination. The U.S. government tried to assassinate Castro three times, once even hiring a mafia hit man to kill him. We know that Castro knew we were doing this. The only explanation for this country being the only one in the world not to have any relations with Castro's Cuba for fifty years is that we will not deal with the man who had our president killed. It makes more sense than the Warren Commission's report!

George H. W. Bush was an adequate president. But he campaigned on, and was elected to carry on, the Reagan ideal of less government, lower taxes, and more individual responsibility. The unlikely result of his failure to accomplish these things was President Bill Clinton.

Clinton campaigned on and delivered a fairly conservative agenda, including a balanced budget and welfare reform. His critics complain that he balanced the budget in part by cutting the military. Well, the military needs cut (see chapter 4). There are over 677 billion people in the world. We will never again win a war by throwing our soldiers at the enemy. The only way we win is with a more advanced military backed up by superior manufacturing capability and better funding. Those things come from a healthy economy, not more soldiers. Of course Clinton was the poster child for character flaws but I don't care how he treated his family. The important thing in this job is whether you hurt or help my country.

George W. Bush wasn't influenced by special interest contributions or political considerations, which proves that there is more to being a good president than an honest desire to do a good job. But then Jimmy Carter had already proven that. George W was given the opportunity to make fiscal responsibility something we would expect from our presidents. When George Washington was elected, almost everyone expected that he would serve for the rest of his life. He could have; he would have been unopposed for as long as he wanted the job. Jefferson too could have had the job for life. The decision these men made to step down after two terms changed what the American people expected out of the office of the president. If Bush would have been the second president in a row to leave office with a balanced budget, it would have been very difficult for his successors not to follow suit. I'm not letting Congress off the hook. I'm blaming Bush for not taking the opportunity to stop them. His failure to be fiscally reasonable let alone responsible did more harm to our country than any president since Lyndon Johnson.

When John Kennedy was assassinated we lost more than a president. Kennedy and Barry Goldwater were friends and they had planned to travel the country together, without speechwriters or makeup artists, debating ideas before the next election. Whoever would have won that election, our country would have gained from that discussion of ideas. Instead, we got Lyndon Baines Johnson and we are still paying for his mistakes. Whatever happened that day in Dallas, it was not what the government tried to tell us happened. At this point, it doesn't matter whether there was a conspiracy to assassinate Kennedy or not. What matters is that there was a cover-up and the government was part of it. It was a symptom of a power other than the States or the People at work in the Federal Government.

Barack Obama would have never been elected if George W. Bush had done even an adequate job. But here we are. The greatest danger facing our country today is the financial insolvency of the government. Barack Obama's budget for his first year in office was four times what Bush's budget was for 2008. In April 2009, when 50 people were diagnosed with swine flu, his immediate knee jerk reaction was to ask Congress for 1.5 billion dollars to fight it. At the rate he is spending he will have by the end of his first term added more to the federal deficit than all previous administrations combined. Nobody thinks this is a good idea, so why is it happening?

In 1960, John F. Kennedy said "ask not what your country can do for you, but what you can do for your country" then he sent legislation to Congress asking that the government do things for the people that the people could and should have done for themselves. This slide toward asking the government to do for us started with Roosevelt and Truman and has chugged along steadily ever since, with only Eisenhower, Ford, Reagan and Clinton even trying to slow it down. Given our current financial condition, the only responsible budget for next year would be a balanced one. If the president submits and Congress passes another deficit budget they are not working in our best interest. They are illegally exercising control over the States and the People.

The American people do not want U.S. troops in 135 foreign countries, we do not want 13 million people entering our country illegally, and we do not want to be 12 trillion dollars in debt. The fact that our government is doing these things anyway proves that they serve somebody else.

Our Founding Fathers knew that capitalism was a necessary part of political freedom. They also knew that if it was to benefit the U.S. economy it had to be U.S. capitalism, so the first tax they imposed was a tariff on imported goods. Today, they make protectionism sound like a dirty word, but if we don't protect American who will?

Today each Congressional seat cost tens of millions of dollars to get and is worth hundreds of millions if you can keep it. Nobody can take this kind of money without owing somebody. The corporations who pay this money may have offices in this country but their interests are global. There is only one reason they give hundreds of millions of dollars to members of Congress each year, to buy the representation that belongs to the American people.

Freddie Mac paid a $3.8 million fine in 2006 for illegally channeling money into the campaigns of more than 50 members of Congress[1]. The same members of Congress who were suppose to be keeping tabs on Fannie Mae and Freddie Mac. In 2008, when the housing market collapsed, these two government-funded companies held almost half, 5.3 trillion dollars worth of all the outstanding mortgage debt in the United States[2]. They lost 50 billion dollars in 2008 alone and we have spent billions of taxpayer dollars to save them from bankruptcy.

From 1989 to 2008, 354 members of Congress took 4.8 million dollars from these two companies. Chris Dodd took the most at $164,500, Barack Obama was second at $126,349 and John Kerry was third having taken $111,000. Hillary Clinton and Nancy Pelosi both made the top 25 taking $76,050 and $56,250 respectively. It wasn't just Democrats. Bob Bennett, Spencer Bachus, Roy Blunt, and Chris Bond were all in the top ten, taking $107,999, $103,300, $96,950 and $95,400[3]. They knew what they were doing. They knew that putting millions of people in debt without the assets back it up would end in disaster. They did it for profit. They are criminals who are above the law and we let them do it.

Ron Paul warned us about this in 2003, the same year John McCain co-sponsored a bill which would have taken supervisory and regulatory authority over Fannie Mae and Freddie Mac away from Congress and given it to the treasury department. By 2008, even Bill Clinton was blaming Congress for resisting efforts by him and some Republicans to tighten up on Fannie Mae and Freddie Mac.

With this lesson barely behind us, you would think that we would make a change before the next bubble burst. But instead, Barack Obama,

Tim Geitner and Congress are intentionally creating the mother of all bubbles, the bankruptcy of the United States government.

FROM THE ASHES

Two days after my ninth birthday Neil Armstrong walked on the moon. That event helped to shape my expectations for the future of this country. Most of the technology developed for years after was a direct result of the research and experience gained from the Apollo project. The return on that investment put the United States of America ahead of the rest of the world economically, militarily and technologically for a generation. Space exploration is one of the few things that the government has proven it can do better than anyone else in the world. The giant leap we took in 1969 should have been the first of many.

40 years later, my son believes that when he grows up he will be wealthy and successful. He is smart, he works hard, he will go to college, he understands the value of honor, but he will not be wealthy and successful. Just like my future in an America where going to the moon was just the first step in the advancement of a society that would do bigger and greater things, his future in an America where a man can work hard and succeed has been stolen. The future we leave his children will be determined by who succeeds the current Congressional regime.

From the beginning of civilization most rulers have claimed their right to rule from god. And for the most part, their subjects went along with it. The concept of a society in which every member has a right to individual liberty did not exist until our Declaration of Independence. And even then it was just an idea. It was not practiced because the idea was so foreign to the minds of even our founders that Thomas Jefferson wrote the Declaration in the comfort and leisure of a man whose hundred or so slaves farmed his land, cleaned his house, and prepared his meals. The concepts that this country was founded on would not be practiced before over six hundred thousand Americans died in the civil war, and then slowly, with each generation moving a little closer to the idea, we became the first society in human history to actually believe in Justice and Liberty for all.

It was not a concept that came easily to the human mind, but once introduced it could be a turning point in the evolution of human society. If freedom and liberty were preserved here, its evolution would continue and it could spread with each successive generation until all people believed that they have the right to be free. Tyrants and dictators would not flourish in that world.

But liberty is dying in America. Freedom comes at a cost; as a slave, you depend on your master for your next meal. Once freed, if you don't feed yourself you will starve. Liberty is the opportunity to secure your next meal. Responsibility and liberty are two sides of the same coin. If you are not responsible for your own decisions, you are not free.

Our government, as a policy, is bringing more Americans every day under its dependency. Under the guise of compassion we are being enslaved. Our founding documents guarantee our liberty, not our next meal. This policy is eroding, and if not stopped will destroy, freedom in this country. The United States of America is more than the first nation in history where individual liberty is guaranteed, it is also a land of natural wonders and resources unparalleled on our planet, where a people may not only be free but wealthy. This country will be the Atlantis of the future, a paradise where the people were free and had every opportunity to wealth, but traded both for a free meal.

The United States Congress is by design a group of people who control varying amounts of the wealth of its citizens. The Constitution that each member swore to defend requires that they act in the interest of the people. But the institution is corrupt. Members use their offices to consolidate power which they use to keep their seats. After decades in office they control one third of the wealth of the nation and the only interest they defend are those of the organizations who have contributed cash to their campaigns funds. They control everything, including the process that was designed to allow us to replace them.

Presidents from both parties have tried and failed to control them. They have turned the tables on the people, who are supposed to hold the power in this Republic. The result was the same as if they would have marched soldiers into Washington and taken it by force.

In 2009 while we were losing our jobs and our retirement funds, Congress gave themselves a three thousand dollar raise. Unfortunately that raise was just misdirection to cover the fact that at the same time they raised their salary to around a hundred seventy five thousand, they raised their expense allotment to about 1.5 million. But that is nothing compared to their 3.1 trillion dollar 2009 budget which included thousands of earmarks totaling billions of dollars and was at least 611 billion more than their over taxation will bring in[1]. That they can get away with using their positions to direct funds they have sworn to protect for their own personal gain is a symptom of how corrupt this institution has become. That they are spending trillions of dollars, and plunging us into a debt that can probably never be repaid is proof that they do not care about the country they have sworn to protect. It is time to admit the truth: the United States Congress is our enemy.

If we make the dishonest choice we will commit at least a generation of Americans to live through an economic collapse that could be worse than the great depression, just to learn that you can't spend yourself out of a recession, and you can't borrow yourself out of debt. Our enemies at home and abroad will try to take advantage of our condition. We will have the same enemies after a collapse of our economic system that we have today. North Korea, Iran, and Al-Qaida will be emboldened by our plight and we will have fewer resources with which to defend ourselves. The two major religions of this world have been at war since the time of Muhammad, but in America Christians and Muslims live with Jews and Atheists in peace. That's why we are a threat to Islamic extremist and it's why Osama bin Laden attacked us on September 11, 2001. And that's why we will prevail if we follow the United States Constitution. As amazing as it is that our founders created a document this powerful, that is as relevant today as it was two hundred years ago, it is more amazing that we have allowed Congress to abandon it.

The same weapon will prevail against domestic threats to the resurrection of our nation. We will win with elections, not guns, with the rule of law and an adherence to the principles that this country was founded on. We lost this country because we traded individual responsibility for a big powerful government. When that government collapses there will be an opportunity for the American people to regain control. It won't happen by itself, we need to be prepared and we need to all be on the same page, the one that starts with "We the People". Our guns are vital to our success because without them we would be crushed under the feet of tyrants and thugs. But we cannot win with violence. The irresponsible use of force would destroy the cause of freedom faster than anything the government could do.

But the fact remains that the Federal Government as it exists today cannot survive. It's math; they simply cannot spend money at the rate they have over the last 10 years without going bankrupt. They are already defaulting on the federal debt and every payment they can't make gets added to the debt, this is the big bubble. They will fail and they will be replaced. The question is how soon and with what.

If they stay in power until our economy crashes, the transition will be difficult and dangerous. And make no mistake, it will be violent. But if we replace them now, before the big bubble burst we can recover more easily and peacefully. The first and most important step is to replace Congress; every member, Democrat and Republican. Then stop asking your Congressmen and Governor to bring home federal dollars. Take care of yourselves and don't ask for or accept any help from the government. This has to be done at the state and individual level, not coincidentally, right where the Constitution says the power and responsibility should be.

After thousands of years of pharaohs, kings, popes, and tyrants claiming divine right to rule, we have found at last the truly sacred rights of freedom and liberty. They are worth fighting for; they are worth dying for if we must. The price of failure is slavery. The rewards for victory will surpass our wildest dreams. Going to the moon really was the first step on a new road that could have lead to a future of unimaginable wealth and opportunity. When we get back on that road, we will be traveling towards a future where our species is more than the smartest animal on the planet. We will learn the secrets of the universe; anything you can imagine is possible. The optimism of youth has a truer vision of the human potential than exist in the minds of today's politicians.

The advances we will make in a few generations will dwarf the jump from black powder to space travel because gains in knowledge increase exponentially. The farther we advance, the faster the next advances come. All we need is the dynamic economy of a free people to fuel it. We will cure disease and poverty. We will discover endless supplies of energy. Through the evolution of ideas as foreign to us as freedom was to our forefathers we will become a better race. We will accomplish things that are beyond our comprehension today. This is the destiny of our people and one generation of selfish greedy people does not have the right to trade it for their short term comfort.

A small group of people can change the future for generations of people. It has happened many times throughout history, but never before have the stakes been this high. The lifetime of a human being is a valuable thing. But the value of life is never improved by anything for which you paid no price. The only thing your government can give you that will add real value to your life is freedom and rules of fair play. The other things that make life worth more, honor, love, faith, pride, wealth, and knowledge, cannot be handed out from above. The more you think you are getting for nothing, the more you are really giving up.

The system that we have allowed our government to devolve into will not survive. The time will come when we will have the opportunity to correct the mistakes that have cost us the future that should have been. But we may need to survive some pretty hard days in the meantime. Being prepared for the worst will make life easier and leave us in a better position to defend our country.

There is one fundamental reason why surviving an economic collapse will require extraordinary preparation: there are too many people. Without a sophisticated social system there is not enough food, water, waste disposal, or room for this many people. If our economic system collapses, there will be millions of desperate people with no food or water and thousands of criminals who will thrive in the chaos. You not only need to have the resources to take care of yourself, you need to be able to defend them.

Millions of Americans started saving guns, ammunition, and non perishable food back in the 1990's because of the Y2K scare. That was a good trial run for the coming economic collapse. It is inevitable and it is not far off. If you still think it is unlikely, prepare anyway. It won't hurt, it may save your life, and could save our country. Making yourself better able to survive in a catastrophe is common sense. If it doesn't happen you will still benefit.

Learn to cook, grow a garden, make beer, hunt, fish, walk in the woods and find out where the food is. Own at least two guns and several thousand rounds of ammunition. Stock up on lighters, candles, flashlights, batteries, boots, outdoor cloths and dry beans and rice. You will have to be able to find water from outside sources but you should have enough for a week or so stored. You can't have too much ammunition, dry beans, and rice. These will be currency if things get bad.

Learn how to take care of yourself and your family. There could be days, even years, when you will not be able to count on having electricity, law enforcement, or grocery stores. Have a plan, prepare a place to defend, and make sure your family knows where to meet in an emergency. Supply lines for food distribution in this country are about three days, the dependence on "just in time" food distribution is why even a predicted snow storm leaves store shelves empty. In a real emergency you will need to be able to feed yourself.

100 percent of the consequences of the actions of this government will fall on the American people. We must prepare to pay for the trillions of dollars that Congress is taking to advance their own power. If you count the 12 Trillion in debts that are on the books, add the 40 or 50 trillion it will take to replace what they stole from Social Security and Medicare, it becomes clear that no one in our government plans on paying any of this back. But there's a catch: it is real spending and it will have real consequences. The transfer has already happened and the effect on our lives will be the same as if they collected it in taxes. The government will absorb enough of the gross domestic product to pay the interest on this debt. Under this massive burden, our economy will no longer operate as the self interested free market system that made us a world power, destroying the only thing that could have saved our economic system.

If you think that this is an extreme prediction that is unlikely to come true, it is because you are under the assumption that for some reason this country is immune to failure. That's the same mistake the Egyptians, Mayans, Romans, and Ottomans made. It is human nature to think that if your nation dominates the world, it always will. But the one thing that every great empire has in common is that they all failed.

This Republic will not survive "just because". It will survive only if we are diligent and responsible as a government and as individuals. The only way to get 300 million individuals to act responsibly is to have a system that rewards responsible behavior and punishes irresponsible behavior. A responsible government would implement that system and would not use it to enrich themselves at the expense of the people they represent. Because this is exactly what's happening in the United States today; failure is not only possible, it's likely.

If our enemies cannot be defeated on Election Day we will be left with only two choices. Abandon all of our descendants to slavery and poverty or fight for our country in the only way that will be left to us. That is for each of us to defend our own individual liberty and to defend the principles in our founding documents from the local and state level. Our country and the justice and liberty for which it stands will survive only if we defend it.

The Declaration of Independence and the Constitution clearly give the people the authority to check excess governmental power, specifically the Right of the People to alter or to abolish it, and to institute new Government. Authority would be worthless without the means to enforce it. The second amendment provides the means for the people to enforce their sovereignty over the government. In order to completely strip us of our freedom, it will be necessary for the government to take this power from us. By depriving us of the last resort to defend individual liberty, they will deprive us of that liberty. If we are going to be in a position to support our Constitution in the future, we must retain the ability to take care of ourselves.

With this power comes responsibility. The greatest threat to lawful gun ownership in this country is the large number of criminals with guns. Every reckless act with a gun puts at risk every citizen's ability to protect themselves. Reasonable regulation, and responsible behavior, is as important to our ability to keep and bear arms as the second amendment itself. The failure to control our southern border is allowing millions of criminals into the country. They are trafficking in drugs, forming gangs, and arming themselves. They are not only a threat to the peace and security of our nation, they are the greatest threat to our right to keep and bear arms. And when the economic collapse disrupts the order of our system, this threat will be on your doorstep.

In 2005 there were an estimated 258 million privately owned guns in the United States[2]. We are the most well armed citizens in the world. 75 million Americans, about half the adult population, keep a private arsenal. In the chaos to come there are 75 million Americans who will be able to defend at least some of their property. This is important because if our system collapses there will be an opportunity to rebuild it, but only if we can preserve the integrity of a large number of free people. Armed with our guns, the Declaration of Independence, the U.S. Constitution, and the sure knowledge that we have a right to be free, we will rise from the ashes that will be left after this unsustainable Congressional regime fails.

MR. / MADAM PRESIDENT, CONGRESSPERSON, SENATOR:

You need to know that we will not sit by while you steal everything our forefathers fought for, everything we have worked a lifetime earning, everything our children will earn in their lifetime, without a fight. You need to understand the seriousness of your crimes, and that there will be consequences. In the end, the American people will prevail. By your peaceful capitulation or by force, but we will win. The only question is how much harm you will do to our country in the mean time.

We do not ask much, just that you be honest. You are spending our money, stop! You are selling our children into slavery, stop!

A Proposed Amendment to the Constitution Requiring a balanced Federal Budget

Resolved by the People of the United States of America. That the following article is proposed as an amendment to the Constitution of the United States, which shall be valid to all intents and purposes as part of the Constitution when ratified by the legislatures of three-fourths of the several States:

SECTION 1. The President shall submit no budget before Congress that exceeds the reasonably expected revenue for the period involved.

SECTION 2. That Congress shall pass no bill whose cost would exceed the reasonably expected revenue for the period involved.

SECTION 3. That the President or Congress can receive an exception to these restrictions only by a two thirds vote of the Governors of the several United States.

Name	Address	Phone	Email

Send signed petitions to Too Great a Nation, P.O. Box 406, Mountain Home, AR 72654

Dan Fragoules

A Proposed Amendment to the Constitution prohibiting Congress from bundling legislation

Resolved by the People of the United States of America. That the following article is proposed as an amendment to the Constitution of the United States, which shall be valid to all intents and purposes as part of the Constitution when ratified by the legislatures of three-fourths of the several States:

SECTION 1. All Congressional appropriations must be voted on and sent to the President individually.

SECTION 2. That Congress shall instruct no spending that is not part of the legislative text of a bill sent to the President. "No earmarks"

Name	Address	Phone	Email

Send signed petitions to Too Great a Nation, P.O. Box 406, Mountain Home, AR 72654

A Proposed Amendment to the Constitution limiting the terms of both Houses of Congress

Resolved by the People of the United States of America. That the following article is proposed as an amendment to the Constitution of the United States, which shall be valid to all intents and purposes as part of the Constitution when ratified by the legislatures of three-fourths of the several States:

SECTION 1. No member of the U.S. House of Representatives shall serve more than four, two year terms.

SECTION 2. No member of the U.S. Senate shall serve more than two, six year terms.

Name	Address	Phone	Email

Send signed petitions to Too Great a Nation, P.O. Box 406, Mountain Home, AR 72654

Dan Fragoules

A Proposed Amendment to the Constitution defining a process for allowing the people to propose popular amendments

Resolved by the People of the United States of America. That the following article is proposed as an amendment to the Constitution of the United States, which shall be valid to all intents and purposes as part of the Constitution when ratified by the legislatures of three-fourths of the several States:

SECTION 1. An amendment to the U.S. Constitution will be referred to the states when a referendum of two percent of the citizens of the United States is submitted.

Name	Address	Phone	Email

Send signed petitions to Too Great a Nation, P.O. Box 406, Mountain Home, AR 72654

A Proposed Amendment to the Constitution clarifying the Federal Government's responsibility concerning the Post Office.

Resolved by the People of the United States of America. That the following article is proposed as an amendment to the Constitution of the United States, which shall be valid to all intents and purposes as part of the Constitution when ratified by the legislatures of three-fourths of the several States:

SECTION 1. The line in Article I Section VIII which grants Congress the power "To establish Post Offices and post Roads" will be amended to state "To regulate and enforce the security of document delivery and transmission within the United States, its territories, and appropriate foreign locations.

Name	Address	Phone	Email

Send signed petitions to Too Great a Nation, P.O. Box 406, Mountain Home, AR 72654

> *"The sacred rights of mankind are not to be rummaged for among old parchments or musty records. They are written, as with a sunbeam, in the whole volume of human nature, by the hand of the divinity itself; and can never be erased."* **- Alexander Hamilton**

IN CONGRESS, July 4, 1776.

The unanimous Declaration of the thirteen united States of America,

When in the Course of human events, it becomes necessary for one people to dissolve the political bands which have connected them with another, and to assume among the powers of the earth, the separate and equal station to which the Laws of Nature and of Nature's God entitle them, a decent respect to the opinions of mankind requires that they should declare the causes which impel them to the separation.

We hold these truths to be self-evident, that all men are created equal, that they are endowed by their Creator with certain unalienable Rights, that among these are Life, Liberty and the pursuit of Happiness.--That to secure these rights, Governments are instituted among Men, deriving their just powers from the consent of the governed, --That whenever any Form of Government becomes destructive of these ends, it is the Right of the People to alter or to abolish it, and to institute new Government, laying its foundation on such principles and organizing its powers in such form, as to them shall seem most likely to effect their Safety and Happiness. Prudence, indeed, will dictate that Governments long established should not be changed for light and transient causes; and accordingly all experience hath shewn, that mankind are more disposed to suffer, while evils are sufferable, than to right themselves by abolishing the forms to which they are accustomed. But when a long train of abuses and usurpations, pursuing invariably the same Object evinces a design to reduce them under absolute Despotism, it is their right, it is their duty, to throw off such Government, and to provide new Guards for their future security.--Such has been the patient sufferance of these Colonies; and such is now the necessity which constrains them to alter their former Systems of Government. The history of the present King of Great Britain is a history of repeated injuries and usurpations, all having in direct object the establishment of an absolute Tyranny over these States. To prove this, let Facts be submitted to a candid world.

He has refused his Assent to Laws, the most wholesome and necessary for the public good.

He has forbidden his Governors to pass Laws of immediate and pressing importance, unless suspended in their operation till his Assent should be obtained; and when so suspended, he has utterly neglected to attend to them.

He has refused to pass other Laws for the accommodation of large districts of people, unless those people would relinquish the right of Representation in the Legislature, a right inestimable to them and formidable to tyrants only.

He has called together legislative bodies at places unusual, uncomfortable, and distant from the depository of their public Records, for the sole purpose of fatiguing them into compliance with his measures.

He has dissolved Representative Houses repeatedly, for opposing with manly firmness his invasions on the rights of the people.

He has refused for a long time, after such dissolutions, to cause others to be elected; whereby the Legislative powers, incapable of Annihilation, have returned to the People at large for their exercise; the State remaining in the mean time exposed to all the dangers of invasion from without, and convulsions within.

He has endeavoured to prevent the population of these States; for that purpose obstructing the Laws for Naturalization of Foreigners; refusing to pass others to encourage their migrations hither, and raising the conditions of new Appropriations of Lands.

He has obstructed the Administration of Justice, by refusing his Assent to Laws for establishing Judiciary powers.

He has made Judges dependent on his Will alone, for the tenure of their offices, and the amount and payment of their salaries.

He has erected a multitude of New Offices, and sent hither swarms of Officers to harrass our people, and eat out their substance.

He has kept among us, in times of peace, Standing Armies without the Consent of our legislatures.

He has affected to render the Military independent of and superior to the Civil power.

He has combined with others to subject us to a jurisdiction foreign to our constitution, and unacknowledged by our laws; giving his Assent to their Acts of pretended Legislation:

For Quartering large bodies of armed troops among us:

For protecting them, by a mock Trial, from punishment for any Murders which they should commit on the Inhabitants of these States:

For cutting off our Trade with all parts of the world:

For imposing Taxes on us without our Consent:

For depriving us in many cases, of the benefits of Trial by Jury:

For transporting us beyond Seas to be tried for pretended offences

For abolishing the free System of English Laws in a neighbouring Province, establishing therein an Arbitrary government, and enlarging its Boundaries so as to render it at once an example and fit instrument for introducing the same absolute rule into these Colonies:

For taking away our Charters, abolishing our most valuable Laws, and altering fundamentally the Forms of our Governments:

For suspending our own Legislatures, and declaring themselves invested with power to legislate for us in all cases whatsoever.

He has abdicated Government here, by declaring us out of his Protection and waging War against us.

He has plundered our seas, ravaged our Coasts, burnt our towns, and destroyed the lives of our people.

He is at this time transporting large Armies of foreign Mercenaries to compleat the works of death, desolation and tyranny, already begun with circumstances of Cruelty & perfidy scarcely paralleled in the most barbarous ages, and totally unworthy the Head of a civilized nation.

He has constrained our fellow Citizens taken Captive on the high Seas to bear Arms against their Country, to become the executioners of their friends and Brethren, or to fall themselves by their Hands.

He has excited domestic insurrections amongst us, and has endeavoured to bring on the inhabitants of our frontiers, the merciless Indian Savages, whose known rule of warfare, is an undistinguished destruction of all ages, sexes and conditions.

In every stage of these Oppressions We have Petitioned for Redress in the most humble terms: Our repeated Petitions have been answered only by repeated injury. A Prince whose character is thus marked by every act which may define a Tyrant, is unfit to be the ruler of a free people.

Nor have We been wanting in attentions to our Brittish brethren. We have warned them from time to time of attempts by their legislature to extend an unwarrantable jurisdiction over us. We have reminded them of the circumstances of our emigration and settlement here. We have appealed to their native justice and magnanimity, and we have conjured them by the ties of our common kindred to disavow these usurpations, which, would inevitably interrupt our connections and correspondence. They too have been deaf to the voice of justice and of consanguinity. We must, therefore, acquiesce in the necessity, which denounces our Separation, and hold them, as we hold the rest of mankind, Enemies in War, in Peace Friends.

We, therefore, the Representatives of the united States of America, in General Congress, Assembled, appealing to the Supreme Judge of the world for the rectitude of our intentions, do, in the Name, and by Authority of the good People of these Colonies, solemnly publish and declare, That these United Colonies are, and of Right ought to be Free and Independent States; that they are Absolved from all Allegiance to the British Crown, and that all political connection between them and the State of Great Britain, is and ought to be totally dissolved; and that as Free and Independent States, they have full Power to levy War, conclude Peace, contract Alliances, establish Commerce, and to do all other Acts and Things which Independent States may of right do. And for the support of this Declaration, with a firm reliance on the protection of divine Providence, we mutually pledge to each other our Lives, our Fortunes and our sacred Honor.

CONSTITUTION FOR THE UNITED STATES OF AMERICA

We the People of the United States, in Order to form a more perfect Union, establish Justice, insure domestic Tranquility, provide for the common defence, promote the general Welfare, and secure the Blessings of Liberty to ourselves and our Posterity, do ordain and establish this Constitution for the United States of America.

Article. I.

Section. 1. All legislative Powers herein granted shall be vested in a Congress of the United States, which shall consist of a Senate and House of Representatives.

Section. 2. The House of Representatives shall be composed of Members chosen every second Year by the People of the several States, and the Electors in each State shall have the Qualifications requisite for Electors of the most numerous Branch of the State Legislature.

No Person shall be a Representative who shall not have attained to the Age of twenty five Years, and been seven Years a Citizen of the United States, and who shall not, when elected, be an Inhabitant of that State in which he shall be chosen.

Representatives and direct Taxes shall be apportioned among the several States which may be included within this Union, according to their respective Numbers, which shall be determined by adding to the whole Number of free Persons, including those bound to Service for a Term of Years, and excluding Indians not taxed, three fifths of all other Persons. (Modified by Amendment

XIV) The actual Enumeration shall be made within three Years after the first Meeting of the Congress of the United States, and within every subsequent Term of ten Years, in such Manner as they shall by Law direct. The Number of Representatives shall not exceed one for every thirty Thousand, but each State shall have at Least one Representative; and until such enumeration shall be made, the State of New Hampshire shall be entitled to chuse three, Massachusetts eight, Rhode-Island and Providence Plantations one, Connecticut five, New-York six, New Jersey four, Pennsylvania eight, Delaware one, Maryland six, Virginia ten, North Carolina five, South Carolina five, and Georgia three.

When vacancies happen in the Representation from any State, the Executive Authority thereof shall issue Writs of Election to fill such Vacancies.

The House of Representatives shall chuse their Speaker and other Officers; and shall have the sole Power of Impeachment.

Section. 3. The Senate of the United States shall be composed of two Senators from each State, *chosen by the Legislature thereof* (Modified by Amendment XVII) for six Years; and each Senator shall have one Vote.

Immediately after they shall be assembled in Consequence of the first Election, they shall be divided as equally as may be into three Classes. The Seats of the Senators of the first Class shall be vacated at the Expiration of the second Year, of the second Class at the Expiration of the fourth Year, and of the third Class at the Expiration of the sixth Year, so that one third may be chosen every second Year; *and if Vacancies happen by Resignation, or otherwise, during the Recess of the Legislature of any State, the Executive thereof may make temporary Appointments until the next Meeting of the Legislature, which shall then fill such Vacancies.* (Modified by Amendment XVII)

No Person shall be a Senator who shall not have attained to the Age of thirty Years, and been nine Years a Citizen of the United States, and who shall not, when elected, be an Inhabitant of that State for which he shall be chosen.

The Vice President of the United States shall be President of the Senate, but shall have no Vote, unless they be equally divided.

The Senate shall chuse their other Officers, and also a President pro tempore, in the Absence of the Vice President, or when he shall exercise the Office of President of the United States.

The Senate shall have the sole Power to try all Impeachments. When sitting for that Purpose, they shall be on Oath or Affirmation. When the President of the United States is tried, the Chief Justice shall preside: And no Person shall be convicted without the Concurrence of two thirds of the Members present.

Judgment in Cases of Impeachment shall not extend further than to removal from Office, and disqualification to hold and enjoy any Office of honor, Trust or Profit under the United States: but the Party convicted shall nevertheless be liable and subject to Indictment, Trial, Judgment and Punishment, according to Law.

Section. 4. The Times, Places and Manner of holding Elections for Senators and Representatives, shall be prescribed in each State by the Legislature thereof; but the Congress may at any time by Law make or alter such Regulations, except as to the Places of chusing Senators.

The Congress shall assemble at least once in every Year, *and such Meeting shall be on the first Monday in December* (Modified by Amendment XX) unless they shall by Law appoint a different Day.

Section. 5. Each House shall be the Judge of the Elections, Returns and Qualifications of its own Members, and a Majority of each shall constitute a Quorum to do Business; but a smaller Number may adjourn from day to day, and may be authorized to compel the Attendance of absent Members, in such Manner, and under such Penalties as each House may provide.

Each House may determine the Rules of its Proceedings, punish its Members for disorderly Behaviour, and, with the Concurrence of two thirds, expel a Member.

Each House shall keep a Journal of its Proceedings, and from time to time publish the same, excepting such Parts as may in their Judgment require Secrecy; and the Yeas and Nays of the Members of either House on any question shall, at the Desire of one fifth of those Present, be entered on the Journal.

Neither House, during the Session of Congress, shall, without the Consent of the other, adjourn for more than three days, nor to any other Place than that in which the two Houses shall be sitting.

Section. 6. The Senators and Representatives shall receive a Compensation for their Services, to be ascertained by Law, and paid out of the Treasury of the United States. They shall in all Cases, except Treason, Felony and Breach of the Peace, be privileged from Arrest during their Attendance at the Session of their respective Houses, and in going to and returning from the same; and for any Speech or Debate in either House, they shall not be questioned in any other Place.

No Senator or Representative shall, during the Time for which he was elected, be appointed to any civil Office under the Authority of the United States, which shall have been created, or the Emoluments whereof shall have been encreased during such time; and no Person holding any Office under the United States, shall be a Member of either House during his Continuance in Office.

Section. 7. All Bills for raising Revenue shall originate in the House of Representatives; but the Senate may propose or concur with Amendments as on other Bills.

Every Bill which shall have passed the House of Representatives and the Senate, shall, before it become a Law, be presented to the President of the United States. If he approve he shall sign it, but if not he shall return it, with his Objections to that House in which it shall have originated, who shall enter the Objections at large on their Journal, and proceed to reconsider it. If after such Reconsideration two thirds of that House shall agree to pass the Bill, it shall be sent, together with the Objections, to the other House, by which it shall likewise be reconsidered, and if approved by two thirds of that House, it shall become a Law. But in all such Cases the Votes of both Houses shall be determined by yeas and Nays, and the Names of the Persons voting for and against the Bill shall be entered on the Journal of each House respectively. If any Bill shall not be returned by the President within ten Days (Sundays excepted) after it shall have been presented to him, the Same shall be a Law, in like Manner as if he had signed it, unless the Congress by their Adjournment prevent its Return, in which Case it shall not be a Law.

Every Order, Resolution, or Vote to which the Concurrence of the Senate and House of Representatives may be necessary (except on a question of Adjournment) shall be presented to the President of the United States; and before the Same shall take Effect, shall be approved by him, or being disapproved by him, shall be repassed by two thirds of the Senate and House of Representatives, according to the Rules and Limitations prescribed in the Case of a Bill.

Section. 8. The Congress shall have Power To lay and collect Taxes, Duties, Imposts and Excises, to pay the Debts and provide for the common Defence and general Welfare of the United States; but all Duties, Imposts and Excises shall be uniform throughout the United States;

To borrow Money on the credit of the United States;

To regulate Commerce with foreign Nations, and among the several States, and with the Indian Tribes;

To establish an uniform Rule of Naturalization, and uniform Laws on the subject of Bankruptcies throughout the United States;

To coin Money, regulate the Value thereof, and of foreign Coin, and fix the Standard of Weights and Measures;

To provide for the Punishment of counterfeiting the Securities and current Coin of the United States;

To establish Post Offices and post Roads;

To promote the Progress of Science and useful Arts, by securing for limited Times to Authors and Inventors the exclusive Right to their respective Writings and Discoveries;

To constitute Tribunals inferior to the supreme Court;

To define and punish Piracies and Felonies committed on the high Seas, and Offences against the Law of Nations;

To declare War, grant Letters of Marque and Reprisal, and make Rules concerning Captures on Land and Water;

To raise and support Armies, but no Appropriation of Money to that Use shall be for a longer Term than two Years;

To provide and maintain a Navy;

To make Rules for the Government and Regulation of the land and naval Forces;

To provide for calling forth the Militia to execute the Laws of the Union, suppress Insurrections and repel Invasions;

To provide for organizing, arming, and disciplining, the Militia, and for governing such Part of them as may be employed in the Service of the United States, reserving to the States respectively, the Appointment of the Officers, and the Authority of training the Militia according to the discipline prescribed by Congress;

To exercise exclusive Legislation in all Cases whatsoever, over such District (not exceeding ten Miles square) as may, by Cession of particular States, and the Acceptance of Congress, become the Seat of the Government of the United States, and to exercise like Authority over all Places purchased by the Consent of the Legislature of the State in which the Same shall be, for the Erection of Forts, Magazines, Arsenals, dock-Yards, and other needful Buildings; — And

To make all Laws which shall be necessary and proper for carrying into Execution the foregoing Powers, and all other Powers vested by this Constitution in the Government of the United States, or in any Department or Officer thereof.

Section. 9. The Migration or Importation of such Persons as any of the States now existing shall think proper to admit, shall not be prohibited by the Congress prior to the Year one thousand eight hundred and eight, but a Tax or duty may be imposed on such Importation, not exceeding ten dollars for each Person.

The Privilege of the Writ of Habeas Corpus shall not be suspended, unless when in Cases of Rebellion or Invasion the public Safety may require it.

No Bill of Attainder or ex post facto Law shall be passed.

No Capitation, or other direct, Tax shall be laid, unless in Proportion to the Census or Enumeration herein before directed to be taken.

No Tax or Duty shall be laid on Articles exported from any State.

No Preference shall be given by any Regulation of Commerce or Revenue to the Ports of one State over those of another; nor shall Vessels bound to, or from, one State, be obliged to enter, clear, or pay Duties in another.

No Money shall be drawn from the Treasury, but in Consequence of Appropriations made by Law; and a regular Statement and Account of the Receipts and Expenditures of all public Money shall be published from time to time.

No Title of Nobility shall be granted by the United States: And no Person holding any Office of Profit or Trust under them, shall, without the Consent of the Congress, accept of any present, Emolument, Office, or Title, of any kind whatever, from any King, Prince, or foreign State.

Section. 10. No State shall enter into any Treaty, Alliance, or Confederation; grant Letters of Marque and Reprisal; coin Money; emit Bills of Credit; make any Thing but gold and silver Coin a Tender in Payment of Debts; pass any Bill of Attainder, ex post facto Law, or Law impairing the Obligation of Contracts, or grant any Title of Nobility.

No State shall, without the Consent of the Congress, lay any Imposts or Duties on Imports or Exports, except what may be absolutely necessary for executing it's inspection Laws; and the net Produce of all Duties and Imposts, laid by any State on Imports or Exports, shall be for the Use of the Treasury of the United States; and all such Laws shall be subject to the Revision and Controul of the Congress.

No State shall, without the Consent of Congress, lay any Duty of Tonnage, keep Troops, or Ships of War in time of Peace, enter into any Agreement or Compact with another State, or with a foreign Power, or engage in War, unless actually invaded, or in such imminent Danger as will not admit of delay.

Article. II.

Section. 1. The executive Power shall be vested in a President of the United States of America. He shall hold his Office during the Term of four Years, and, together with the Vice President, chosen for the same Term, be elected, as follows:

Each State shall appoint, in such Manner as the Legislature thereof may direct, a Number of Electors, equal to the whole Number of Senators and Representatives to which the State may be entitled in the Congress: but no Senator or Representative, or Person holding an Office of Trust or Profit under the United States, shall be appointed an Elector.

The Electors shall meet in their respective States, and vote by Ballot for two Persons, of whom one at least shall not be an Inhabitant of the same State with themselves. And they shall make a List of all the Persons voted for, and of the Number of Votes for each; which List they shall sign and certify, and transmit sealed to the Seat of the Government of the United States, directed to the President of the Senate. The President of the Senate shall, in the Presence of the Senate and House of Representatives, open all the Certificates, and the Votes shall then be counted. The Person having the greatest Number of Votes shall be the President, if such Number be a Majority of the whole Number of Electors appointed; and if there be more than one who have such Majority, and have an equal Number of Votes, then the House of Representatives shall immediately chuse by Ballot one of them for President; and if no Person have a Majority, then from the five highest on the List the said House shall in like Manner chuse the President. But in chusing the President, the Votes shall be taken by States, the Representation from each State having one Vote; a quorum for this Purpose shall consist of a Member or Members from two thirds of the States, and a Majority of all the States shall be necessary to a Choice. In every Case, after the Choice of the President, the Person having the greatest Number of Votes of the Electors shall be the Vice President. But if there should remain two or more who have equal Votes, the Senate shall chuse from them by Ballot the Vice President. (Modified by Amendment XII)

The Congress may determine the Time of chusing the Electors, and the Day on which they shall give their Votes; which Day shall be the same throughout the United States.

No Person except a natural born Citizen, or a Citizen of the United States, at the time of the Adoption of this Constitution, shall be eligible to the Office of President; neither shall any Person be eligible to that Office who shall not have attained to the Age of thirty five Years, and been fourteen Years a Resident within the United States.

In Case of the Removal of the President from Office, or of his Death, Resignation, or Inability to discharge the Powers and Duties of the said Office, the Same shall devolve on the Vice President, and the Congress may by Law provide for the Case of Removal, Death, Resignation or Inability, both of the President and Vice President, declaring what Officer shall then act as President, and such Officer shall act accordingly, until the Disability be removed, or a President shall be elected. (Modified by Amendment XXV)

The President shall, at stated Times, receive for his Services, a Compensation, which shall neither be increased nor diminished during the Period for which he shall have been elected, and he shall not receive within that Period any other Emolument from the United States, or any of them.

Before he enter on the Execution of his Office, he shall take the following Oath or Affirmation: — "I do solemnly swear (or affirm) that I will faithfully execute the Office of President of the United States, and will to the best of my Ability, preserve, protect and defend the Constitution of the United States."

Section. 2. The President shall be Commander in Chief of the Army and Navy of the United States, and of the Militia of the several States, when called into the actual Service of the United States; he may require the Opinion, in writing, of the principal Officer in each of the executive Departments, upon any Subject relating to the Duties of their respective Offices, and he shall have Power to grant Reprieves and Pardons for Offences against the United States, except in Cases of Impeachment.

He shall have Power, by and with the Advice and Consent of the Senate, to make Treaties, provided two thirds of the Senators present concur; and he shall nominate, and by and with the Advice and Consent of the Senate, shall appoint Ambassadors, other public Ministers and Consuls, Judges of the supreme Court, and all other Officers of the United States, whose Appointments are not herein otherwise provided for, and which shall be established by Law: but the Congress may by Law vest the Appointment of such inferior Officers, as they think proper, in the President alone, in the Courts of Law, or in the Heads of Departments.

The President shall have Power to fill up all Vacancies that may happen during the Recess of the Senate, by granting Commissions which shall expire at the End of their next Session.

Section. 3. He shall from time to time give to the Congress Information of the State of the Union, and recommend to their Consideration such Measures as he shall judge necessary and expedient; he may, on extraordinary Occasions, convene both Houses, or either of them, and in Case of Disagreement between them, with Respect to the Time of Adjournment, he may adjourn them to such Time as he shall think proper; he shall receive Ambassadors and other public Ministers; he shall take Care that the Laws be faithfully executed, and shall Commission all the Officers of the United States.

Section. 4. The President, Vice President and all civil Officers of the United States, shall be removed from Office on Impeachment for, and Conviction of, Treason, Bribery, or other high Crimes and Misdemeanors.

Article. III.

Section. 1. The judicial Power of the United States shall be vested in one supreme Court, and in such inferior Courts as the Congress may from time to time ordain and establish. The Judges, both of the supreme and inferior Courts, shall hold their Offices during good Behaviour, and shall, at stated Times, receive for their Services a Compensation, which shall not be diminished during their Continuance in Office.

Section. 2. The judicial Power shall extend to all Cases, in Law and Equity, arising under this Constitution, the Laws of the United States, and Treaties made, or which shall be made, under their Authority; — to all Cases affecting Ambassadors, other public Ministers and Consuls; — to all Cases of admiralty and maritime Jurisdiction; — to Controversies to which the United States shall be a Party; — to Controversies between two or more States; — *between a State and Citizens of another State* (Modified by Amendment XI) — between Citizens of different States; — between Citizens of the same State claiming Lands under Grants of different States, and between a State, or the Citizens thereof, and foreign States, Citizens or Subjects.

In all Cases affecting Ambassadors, other public Ministers and Consuls, and those in which a State shall be Party, the supreme Court shall have original Jurisdiction. In all the other Cases before mentioned, the supreme Court shall have appellate Jurisdiction, both as to Law and Fact, with such Exceptions, and under such Regulations as the Congress shall make.

The Trial of all Crimes, except in Cases of Impeachment, shall be by Jury; and such Trial shall be held in the State where the said

Crimes shall have been committed; but when not committed within any State, the Trial shall be at such Place or Places as the Congress may by Law have directed.

Section. 3. Treason against the United States shall consist only in levying War against them, or in adhering to their Enemies, giving them Aid and Comfort. No Person shall be convicted of Treason unless on the Testimony of two Witnesses to the same overt Act, or on Confession in open Court.

The Congress shall have Power to declare the Punishment of Treason, but no Attainder of Treason shall work Corruption of Blood, or Forfeiture except during the Life of the Person attainted.

Article. IV.

Section. 1. Full Faith and Credit shall be given in each State to the public Acts, Records, and judicial Proceedings of every other State. And the Congress may by general Laws prescribe the Manner in which such Acts, Records and Proceedings shall be proved, and the Effect thereof.

Section. 2. The Citizens of each State shall be entitled to all Privileges and Immunities of Citizens in the several States.

A Person charged in any State with Treason, Felony, or other Crime, who shall flee from Justice, and be found in another State, shall on Demand of the executive Authority of the State from which he fled, be delivered up, to be removed to the State having Jurisdiction of the Crime.

No Person held to Service or Labour in one State, under the Laws thereof, escaping into another, shall, in Consequence of any Law or Regulation therein, be discharged from such Service or Labour, but shall be delivered up on Claim of the Party to whom such Service or Labour may be due (Modified by Amendment XIII)

Section. 3. New States may be admitted by the Congress into this Union; but no new State shall be formed or erected within the Jurisdiction of any other State; nor any State be formed by the Junction of two or more States, or Parts of States, without the Consent of the Legislatures of the States concerned as well as of the Congress.

The Congress shall have Power to dispose of and make all needful Rules and Regulations respecting the Territory or other Property belonging to the United States; and nothing in this Constitution shall be so construed as to Prejudice any Claims of the United States, or of any particular State.

Section. 4. The United States shall guarantee to every State in this Union a Republican Form of Government, and shall protect each of them against Invasion; and on Application of the Legislature, or of the Executive (when the Legislature cannot be convened), against domestic Violence.

Article.V.

The Congress, whenever two thirds of both Houses shall deem it necessary, shall propose Amendments to this Constitution, or, on the Application of the Legislatures of two thirds of the several States, shall call a Convention for proposing Amendments, which, in either Case, shall be valid to all Intents and Purposes, as Part of this Constitution, when ratified by the Legislatures of three fourths of the several States, or by Conventions in three fourths thereof, as the one or the other Mode of Ratification may be proposed by the Congress; Provided that no Amendment which may be made prior to the Year One thousand eight hundred and eight shall in any Manner affect the first and fourth Clauses in the Ninth Section of the first Article; *and that no State, without its Consent, shall be deprived of its equal Suffrage in the Senate* (Possibly abrogated by Amendment XVII)

Article.VI.

All Debts contracted and Engagements entered into, before the Adoption of this Constitution, shall be as valid against the United States under this Constitution, as under the Confederation.

This Constitution, and the Laws of the United States which shall be made in Pursuance thereof; and all Treaties made, or which shall be made, under the Authority of the United States, shall be the supreme Law of the Land; and the Judges in every State shall be bound thereby, any Thing in the Constitution or Laws of any State to the Contrary notwithstanding.

The Senators and Representatives before mentioned, and the Members of the several State Legislatures, and all executive and judicial Officers, both of the United States and of the several States, shall be bound by Oath or Affirmation, to support this Constitution; but no religious Test shall ever be required as a Qualification to any Office or public Trust under the United States.

Article.VII.

The Ratification of the Conventions of nine States, shall be sufficient for the Establishment of this Constitution between the States so ratifying the Same.

Bill of Rights and later Amendments

Amendment 1

Congress shall make no law respecting an establishment of religion, or prohibiting the free exercise thereof; or abridging the freedom of speech, or of the press; or the right of the people peaceably to assemble, and to petition the Government for a redress of grievances.

Amendment 2

A well regulated Militia, being necessary to the security of a free State, the right of the people to keep and bear Arms, shall not be infringed.

Amendment 3

No Soldier shall, in time of peace be quartered in any house, without the consent of the Owner, nor in time of war, but in a manner to be prescribed by law.

Amendment 4

The right of the people to be secure in their persons, houses, papers, and effects, against unreasonable searches and seizures, shall not be violated, and no Warrants shall issue, but upon probable cause, supported by Oath or affirmation, and particularly describing the place to be searched, and the persons or things to be seized.

Amendment 5

No person shall be held to answer for a capital, or otherwise infamous crime, unless on a presentment or indictment of a Grand Jury, except in cases arising in the land or naval forces, or in the Militia, when in actual service in time of War or public danger; nor shall any person be subject for the same offense to be twice put in jeopardy of life or limb; nor shall be compelled in any criminal case to be a witness against himself, nor be deprived of life, liberty, or property, without due process of law; nor shall private property be taken for public use, without just compensation.

Amendment 6

In all criminal prosecutions, the accused shall enjoy the right to a speedy and public trial, by an impartial jury of the State and district wherein the crime shall have been committed, which district shall have been previously ascertained by law, and to be informed of the nature and cause of the accusation; to be confronted with the witnesses against him; to have compulsory process for obtaining witnesses in his favor, and to have the Assistance of Counsel for his defence.

Amendment 7

In Suits at common law, where the value in controversy shall exceed twenty dollars, the right of trial by jury shall be preserved, and no fact tried by a jury, shall be otherwise re-examined in any Court of the United States, than according to the rules of the common law.

Amendment 8

Excessive bail shall not be required, nor excessive fines imposed, nor cruel and unusual punishments inflicted.

Amendment 9

The enumeration in the Constitution, of certain rights, shall not be construed to deny or disparage others retained by the people.

Dan Fragoules

Amendment 10

The powers not delegated to the United States by the Constitution, nor prohibited by it to the States, are reserved to the States respectively, or to the people.

Amendment 11

The Judicial power of the United States shall not be construed to extend to any suit in law or equity, commenced or prosecuted against one of the United States by Citizens of another State, or by Citizens or Subjects of any Foreign State.

Amendment 12

The Electors shall meet in their respective states, and vote by ballot for President and Vice-President, one of whom, at least, shall not be an inhabitant of the same state with themselves; they shall name in their ballots the person voted for as President, and in distinct ballots the person voted for as Vice-President, and they shall make distinct lists of all persons voted for as President, and of all persons voted for as Vice-President and of the number of votes for each, which lists they shall sign and certify, and transmit sealed to the seat of the government of the United States, directed to the President of the Senate;

The President of the Senate shall, in the presence of the Senate and House of Representatives, open all the certificates and the votes shall then be counted;

The person having the greatest Number of votes for President, shall be the President, if such number be a majority of the whole number of Electors appointed; and if no person have such majority, then from the persons having the highest numbers not exceeding three on the list of those voted for as President, the House of Representatives shall choose immediately, by ballot, the President. But in choosing the President, the votes shall be taken by states, the representation from each state having one vote; a quorum for this purpose shall consist of a member or members from two-thirds of the states, and a majority of all the states shall be necessary to a choice. And if the House of Representatives shall not choose a President whenever the right of choice shall devolve upon them, before the fourth day of March next following, then the Vice-President shall act as President, as in the case of the death or other constitutional disability of the President.

The person having the greatest number of votes as Vice-President, shall be the Vice-President, if such number be a majority of the whole number of Electors appointed, and if no person have a majority, then from the two highest numbers on the list, the Senate shall choose the Vice-President; a quorum for the purpose shall consist of two-thirds of the whole number of Senators, and a majority of the whole number shall be necessary to a choice. But no person constitutionally ineligible to the office of President shall be eligible to that of Vice-President of the United States.

Amendment 13

1. Neither slavery nor involuntary servitude, except as a punishment for crime whereof the party shall have been duly convicted, shall exist within the United States, or any place subject to their jurisdiction.

2. Congress shall have power to enforce this article by appropriate legislation.

Amendment 14

1. All persons born or naturalized in the United States, and subject to the jurisdiction thereof, are citizens of the United States and of the State wherein they reside. No State shall make or enforce any law which shall abridge the privileges or immunities of citizens of the United States; nor shall any State deprive any person of life, liberty, or property, without due process of law; nor deny to any person within its jurisdiction the equal protection of the laws.

2. Representatives shall be apportioned among the several States according to their respective numbers, counting the whole number of persons in each State, excluding Indians not taxed. But when the right to vote at any election for the choice of electors for President and Vice-President of the United States,

Representatives in Congress, the Executive and Judicial officers of a State, or the members of the Legislature thereof, is denied to any of the male inhabitants of such State, being twenty-one years of age, and citizens of the United States, or in any way abridged, except for participation in rebellion, or other crime, the basis of representation therein shall be reduced in the proportion which the number of such male citizens shall bear to the whole number of male citizens twenty-one years of age in such State.

3. No person shall be a Senator or Representative in Congress, or elector of President and Vice-President, or hold any office, civil or military, under the United States, or under any State, who, having previously taken an oath, as a member of Congress, or as an officer of the United States, or as a member of any State legislature, or as an executive or judicial officer of any State, to support the Constitution of the United States, shall have engaged in insurrection or rebellion against the same, or given aid or comfort to the enemies thereof. But Congress may by a vote of two-thirds of each House, remove such disability.

4. The validity of the public debt of the United States, authorized by law, including debts incurred for payment of pensions and bounties for services in suppressing insurrection or rebellion, shall not be questioned. But neither the United States nor any State shall assume or pay any debt or obligation incurred in aid of insurrection or rebellion against the United States, or any claim for the loss or emancipation of any slave; but all such debts, obligations and claims shall be held illegal and void.

5. The Congress shall have power to enforce, by appropriate legislation, the provisions of this article.

Amendment 15

1. The right of citizens of the United States to vote shall not be denied or abridged by the United States or by any State on account of race, color, or previous condition of servitude.

2. The Congress shall have power to enforce this article by appropriate legislation.

Amendment 16

The Congress shall have power to lay and collect taxes on incomes, from whatever source derived, without apportionment among the several States, and without regard to any census or enumeration.

Amendment 17

The Senate of the United States shall be composed of two Senators from each State, elected by the people thereof, for six years; and each Senator shall have one vote. The electors in each State shall have the qualifications requisite for electors of the most numerous branch of the State legislatures.

When vacancies happen in the representation of any State in the Senate, the executive authority of such State shall issue writs of election to fill such vacancies: Provided, That the legislature of any State may empower the executive thereof to make temporary appointments until the people fill the vacancies by election as the legislature may direct.

This amendment shall not be so construed as to affect the election or term of any Senator chosen before it becomes valid as part of the Constitution.

Amendment 18

1. After one year from the ratification of this article the manufacture, sale, or transportation of intoxicating liquors

within, the importation thereof into, or the exportation thereof from the United States and all territory subject to the jurisdiction thereof for beverage purposes is hereby prohibited.

2. The Congress and the several States shall have concurrent power to enforce this article by appropriate legislation.

3. This article shall be inoperative unless it shall have been ratified as an amendment to the Constitution by the legislatures of the several States, as provided in the Constitution, within seven years from the date of the submission hereof to the States by the Congress.

Amendment 19

The right of citizens of the United States to vote shall not be denied or abridged by the United States or by any State on account of sex.

Congress shall have power to enforce this article by appropriate legislation.

Amendment 20

1. The terms of the President and Vice President shall end at noon on the 20th day of January, and the terms of Senators and Representatives at noon on the 3d day of January, of the years in which such terms would have ended if this article had not been ratified; and the terms of their successors shall then begin.

2. The Congress shall assemble at least once in every year, and such meeting shall begin at noon on the 3d day of January, unless they shall by law appoint a different day.

3. If, at the time fixed for the beginning of the term of the President, the President elect shall have died, the Vice President elect shall become President. If a President shall not have been chosen before the time fixed for the beginning of his term, or if the President elect shall have failed to qualify, then the Vice

President elect shall act as President until a President shall have qualified; and the Congress may by law provide for the case wherein neither a President elect nor a Vice President elect shall have qualified, declaring who shall then act as President, or the manner in which one who is to act shall be selected, and such person shall act accordingly until a President or Vice President shall have qualified.

4. The Congress may by law provide for the case of the death of any of the persons from whom the House of Representatives may choose a President whenever the right of choice shall have devolved upon them, and for the case of the death of any of the persons from whom the Senate may choose a Vice President whenever the right of choice shall have devolved upon them.

5. Sections 1 and 2 shall take effect on the 15th day of October following the ratification of this article.

6. This article shall be inoperative unless it shall have been ratified as an amendment to the Constitution by the legislatures of three-fourths of the several States within seven years from the date of its submission.

Amendment 21

1. The eighteenth article of amendment to the Constitution of the United States is hereby repealed.

2. The transportation or importation into any State, Territory, or possession of the United States for delivery or use therein of intoxicating liquors, in violation of the laws thereof, is hereby prohibited.

3. The article shall be inoperative unless it shall have been ratified as an amendment to the Constitution by conventions in the several States, as provided in the Constitution, within seven years from the date of the submission hereof to the States by the Congress.

Dan Fragoules

Amendment 22

1. No person shall be elected to the office of the President more than twice, and no person who has held the office of President, or acted as President, for more than two years of a term to which some other person was elected President shall be elected to the office of the President more than once. But this Article shall not apply to any person holding the office of President, when this Article was proposed by the Congress, and shall not prevent any person who may be holding the office of President, or acting as President, during the term within which this Article becomes operative from holding the office of President or acting as President during the remainder of such term.

2. This article shall be inoperative unless it shall have been ratified as an amendment to the Constitution by the legislatures of three-fourths of the several States within seven years from the date of its submission to the States by the Congress.

Amendment 23

1. The District constituting the seat of Government of the United States shall appoint in such manner as the Congress may direct: A number of electors of President and Vice President equal to the whole number of Senators and Representatives in Congress to which the District would be entitled if it were a State, but in no event more than the least populous State; they shall be in addition to those appointed by the States, but they shall be considered, for the purposes of the election of President and Vice President, to be electors appointed by a State; and they shall meet in the District and perform such duties as provided by the twelfth article of amendment.

2. The Congress shall have power to enforce this article by appropriate legislation.

Amendment 24

1. The right of citizens of the United States to vote in any primary or other election for President or Vice President, for electors for President or Vice President, or for Senator or Representative in Congress, shall not be denied or abridged by the United States or any State by reason of failure to pay any poll tax or other tax.

2. The Congress shall have power to enforce this article by appropriate legislation.

Amendment 25

1. In case of the removal of the President from office or of his death or resignation, the Vice President shall become President.

2. Whenever there is a vacancy in the office of the Vice President, the President shall nominate a Vice President who shall take office upon confirmation by a majority vote of both Houses of Congress.

3. Whenever the President transmits to the President pro tempore of the Senate and the Speaker of the House of Representatives his written declaration that he is unable to discharge the powers and duties of his office, and until he transmits to them a written declaration to the contrary, such powers and duties shall be discharged by the Vice President as Acting President.

4. Whenever the Vice President and a majority of either the principal officers of the executive departments or of such other body as Congress may by law provide, transmit to the President pro tempore of the Senate and the Speaker of the House of Representatives their written declaration that the President is unable to discharge the powers and duties of his office, the Vice President shall immediately assume the powers and duties of the office as Acting President.

Thereafter, when the President transmits to the President pro tempore of the Senate and the Speaker of the House of Representatives his written declaration that no inability exists, he shall resume the powers and duties of his office unless the Vice President and a majority of either the principal officers of the executive department or of such other body as Congress may by law provide, transmit within four days to the President pro tempore of the Senate and the Speaker of the House of Representatives their written declaration that the President is unable to discharge the powers and duties of his office. Thereupon Congress shall decide the issue, assembling within forty eight hours for that purpose if not in session. If the Congress, within twenty one days after receipt of the latter written declaration, or, if Congress is not in session, within twenty one days after Congress is required to assemble, determines by two thirds vote of both Houses that the President is unable to discharge the powers and duties of his office, the Vice President shall continue to discharge the same as Acting President; otherwise, the President shall resume the powers and duties of his office.

Amendment 26

1. The right of citizens of the United States, who are eighteen years of age or older, to vote shall not be denied or abridged by the United States or by any State on account of age.

2. The Congress shall have power to enforce this article by appropriate legislation.

Amendment 27

No law, varying the compensation for the services of the Senators and Representatives, shall take effect, until an election of Representatives shall have intervened.

The beginning

REFERENCES:

Chapter One, The Honest Choice.

1. Manufacturing & Technology News, June 21, 2006.
2. Data released by the Federal Election Commission on August 23, 2009.

Chapter Two, Spending and Taxes.

1. Government Printing Office and Office of Management and Budget.
2. Joint Economic Committee, 106th Congress, April 2000. Office of Management and Budget, Budget of U.S. Government, February, 2000.
3. Social Security Administration. Internal payroll records.
4. Congressional Budget Office.
5. Social Security Amendments, House Bill H1787 and Senate Bill S4101 April 1983
6. Calculated from data in the 2009 Social Security and Medicare Trustees Report.
7. Internal payroll records.

Chapter Three, The Economy.

1. Data released by the Federal Election Commission, May, 2009 (Published by The Center for Responsive Politics)

2. University of Maryland School of Business.

3. U.S. Department of Energy, Energy Information Agency.

4. Estimate based on information published in The New York Times June 11, 2006 and The Christian Science Monitor March 2007.

5. Manufacturing and Technology News, June, 2006

6. Már Gudmundsson is the Deputy Head of the Monetary and Economic Department of the Bank for International Settlements

7. New York State Comptrollers office, Released January, 2009.

8. Heritage Foundation, James Sherk.

9. U.S. Census Bureau September 2009

10. New York Times Business Section April 2009

11. Consumer Reports February 2009

12. According to a June 4, 2009 study by the Harvard Medical School.

Chapter Four, Energy, Foreign Policy, and Immigration.

1. Data released by the Federal Election Commission, May, 2009 (Published by The Center for Responsive Politics)

2. Statistics released by Rep. Steve King R-Iowa

3. Indiana University-Purdue University Indianapolis, Indiana Dept. of Biology.

Chapter Five, The Third Branch.

  1. Point of Law.com

  2. Towers Perrin Tillinghast (TPT) 2008 Update on U.S. Tort Cost trends.

Chapter Six, History.

  1. Documents released by the Federal Election Commission April, 2006

  2. CNNMoney.com July 2008.

  3. Center for Responsive Politics Sept 2008.

Chapter Seven, From the Ashes.

  1. Office of Management and Budget, Budget of the United States Feb, 2009.

  2. National Academy of Sciences Report, 2004.

It is my hope that this book will change a mind or two if not our country. Failing that let it stand as a confession to our children so they will know just what we got for their liberty.

If it does this in fairly correct and legible English it is because of the coaching, editing, and influence of Julie, Sue and Alex. Thanks for your help.

Printed in the United States
by Baker & Taylor Publisher Services

Printed in the United States
by Baker & Taylor Publisher Services